Endorseme

"Have we ever seen such a rich DNA resource with such crucial insights and global implications for the Kingdom of God in Christ? This discussion belongs to all reflective practitioners and grassroots servants who grapple with the ongoing challenge of narrating to every person in every generation in every geography and in every culture and in their mother tongue, the inexpressible power of the captivating Story of the transforming Servant King. Why did we not have this relatively small publication, packed with vast and true implications, decades ago?"

- William D. Taylor, Senior Mentor, Mission Commission, World Evangelical Alliance

"*Kerugma* (Greek) is the preached word and *Katib* (Hebrew) is the written word. Both are inseparable. The preached word often proceeds before the written word. It is a truism in antiquity as well as in postmodernity. The making and receiving of sound begins the journey of a person's life in birth, and hearing is often the last sense that a person loses before death. Hence, orality and narrative form the basic fabric of a person's learning. It happens in a child's learning (pedagogue) as well as in adult's learning (androgogue). It is true for the tribal people as well as for the technical professionals. The Consultation on Orality at the Billy Graham Center with verbal interactions and the subsequent proceeding in the written form of the present book testify to this paradigmatic shift in missiological thinking. I am honored to witness both events."

- Peter Au, Principal of Canadian Chinese School of Theology at Tyndale University College & Seminary

"Well over 60% of the Bible is dramatic narratives that have been told and retold over the generations as the transformational stories that they are meant to be. In this generation, we are again recovering the importance of this oral communal story-telling of God's word if we are to reach the unreached people of the world, as well as today's digital generation. God's stories told using appropriate cultural art forms and cutting-edge media enable the word of God to bring transformation in the lives of individuals and reformation to every sphere of society. The insights gained through this record of the orality consultation will encourage you to rethink how we might best reengage theological education and training in a fresh way!"

- David Joel Hamilton, Vice President for Strategic Innovation, University of the Nations

"The sweet breeze of loving all of our neighbors is coming from seminaries worldwide. These influencers of higher education are seriously embracing the value of including the needs of oral learners in seminary education. Oral strategies are being examined and included as academics are seeing that this embrace does not have to compromise the supremacy of scripture nor the delivery of theological truth."

- **Dorothy A. Miller, Executive Director, The God's Story Project**

"Oral preference learners are in our midst, for too long we have ignored them and have not figured out how to embrace them in theological education. This book raises thoughtful questions as to our education models, processes, and evaluations. Time has come for us to examine our approaches."

- **Joshua Cho, President, Hong Kong Baptist Theological Seminary**

"Seventy to 80 percent of the world can't, won't, or don't depend on literacy; oral learners do not adequately comprehend nor significantly retain vital information presented to them in literate ways. Therefore, there is great urgency to communicate the truth of the Bible in an understandable way to such precious people in this new century. The chapters presented in this book seek to grapple with critical matters and strategies of theological education and the oral preference learner with a view toward effectiveness in world evangelization."

- **Michael Y. Oh, Executive Director / CEO, The Lausanne Movement**

"The nurture of emerging Christian leaders requires thoughtful and intentional integration of multiple disciplines in the learning and communication processes. *Beyond Literate Western Models* helpfully examines the active intersections of theological education and oral-preference learners around the world. I particularly appreciate the work's implicit summons to the seminary to engage intentionally the need for theologically-rooted trainers of trainers and to equip such people for optimal service in orality contexts."

- **David A. Baer, President & CEO, Overseas Council**

"At last, there is "field manual" for those who see the urgency of effectively communicating basic Christian theology among oral learners. Beyond Literate Western Models, edited by Grant Lovejoy and Samuel Chiang, is precisely the introduction needed for those who realize that the Great Commission's fulfillment demands oral transmission of the deeper theological principles embedded in scripture. This is not simply another overview of commonly known issues associated with the subject of orality. This is a serious "how to" book that will be of great use for years to come. It is a book that will equip us to reach over half the world's population with the full message of the Bible."

- Tom Elliff, President, International Mission Board, Southern Baptist Convention

"As a missiologist and as a father whose daughter is serving a people group in Tanzania with a completely oral culture, I cannot express strongly enough how significant this initiative is to reach the oral-based cultures of the world. This collection of essays covers a wide range of issues, including methods, pedagogy, the relationship of non-formal education to traditional formal programs, and the importance of the narrative structure of the Bible, just to name a few. These essays harvest the best insights from the 2012 Orality Consultation by bringing into one volume experts from across the world. I commend this volume to the Global Church and urge churches and mission agencies everywhere to take up this challenge with vigor. There are thousands of people groups around the world who will not be reached without it."

- Timothy C. Tennent, President and Professor of World Christianity, Asbury Theological Seminary

Beyond Literate Western Models: Contextualizing Theological Education in Oral Contexts

Edited by

Samuel E. Chiang and Grant Lovejoy

Beyond Literate Western Models:
Contextualizing Theological
Education in Oral Contexts

This edition published by International Orality Network
In cooperation with Capstone Enterprises Ltd., Hong Kong

Graphic Design: Cindy Morris, ProPlan, Inc.

Copyright © 2013

International Orality Network

ISBN 962-7673-25-0
Printed in Hong Kong

My people, hear my teaching;
listen to the words of my mouth.
I will open my mouth with a parable;
I will utter hidden things, things from of old—
things we have heard and known,
things our ancestors have told us.
We will not hide them from their descendants;
we will tell the next generation
the praiseworthy deeds of the Lord,
his power, and the wonders he has done.

Psalm 78:1-4 (NIV)

CONTENTS

IMPORTANT WORD

Host Comments for the Consultation on Orality
Summer 2012

Lonnie J. Allison

The Billy Graham Center at Wheaton College, USA, was privileged to host the orality consultation during the summer of 2012. Samuel Chiang and the organizing team brought together many of the world's best thinker-practitioners on this urgent topic.

As I read some of the papers from the consultation, I couldn't help but think, *This consultation was one of the key reasons Billy Graham envisioned the Graham Center.* In the afterglow of the first great Lausanne Congress on World Evangelization in 1974, Dr. Graham saw the need for a "nerve center" for ongoing strategic thinking on missional issues raised by the Global Church community. Wheaton College understood and endorsed his dream and together they built and have sustained the Center since the mid-1970s.

At its best, the Billy Graham Center combines a commitment to thinking that leads to action in the disciplines of biblical and systematic theology, Christian formation, missions, and especially evangelism. Since its founding, the Center has hosted nearly 300 such consultations and conferences, housed a world-class archives and missions and evangelism library, and maintained the Museum of American Evangelism, where more than one million visitors have seen how the gospel of Jesus Christ was planted on American soil from its inception. Nearly 10,000 visitors have made spiritual decisions through the witness of the museum. The building also hosts the Wheaton College Graduate Programs, where each year nearly 500 students, many from the Majority World, come to be trained in the great disciplines of Christian mission.

The orality consultation was of special importance to me and our Graham Center team. It is clear that oral communication is the primary and most accessible way that billions of yet-to-be-reached people can receive the gospel and understand its saving and sanctifying power. This in no way minimizes the high value of placing the scriptures into written languages. Rather, it reminds us of the urgency of the hour. If it is true that every second five people are born and two die in the world, then by all and every means we must speak the gospel with increasing cultural clarity everywhere. I commend this excellent resource to guide indigenous and missional believers in this task, for "how will they hear unless someone tells them?"

FOREWORD

Doug Birdsall

The Lausanne Movement was initiated through the global leadership of Billy Graham and John Stott and their vision to call the *whole Church to take the gospel to the whole world.*

Samuel Chiang is one of the most creative and dynamic leaders in Lausanne in this current era as we work out the priorities of the *Cape Town 2010* Congress and the priorities of the *Cape Town Commitment.*

I will never forget the encounter I had with Avery Willis, Steve Douglass, Paul Eshleman, and a few other global mission leaders when they literally came running into my office during the Lausanne 2004 Forum in Pattaya, Thailand. They wanted to know if they could establish a new network within the Lausanne Movement that would unite and focus the energy and resources of their colleagues who were beginning to discover the significance of a new mission frontier. With a sense of excitement that was reminiscent of a group of schoolboys starting a new club, these globally influential leaders wanted to know what we should call this new group! Their excitement was an expression of their conviction that a united effort would result in breakthroughs on this new frontier in world evangelization.

Their excitement and conviction were well founded. The new frontier is *orality*. Their vision has given birth to an ever-expanding movement within the broader context of the Lausanne Movement. Mission organizations, colleges and seminaries, and churches around the world are catching the vision. In his leadership role as the Lausanne Senior Associate for Orality, Samuel Chiang is leading the way. He, along with his global colleagues, are developing a paradigm that revolutionizes the way in which the Church understands how the majority of the world's people acquire and process information. The Lausanne Movement recognizes Chiang as the authoritative evangelical voice and the strategic leader on orality.

Chiang and Grant Lovejoy share with us the astounding reality that there are an estimated 5.7 billion people who are oral learners. Until recently, the vast majority of mission work has been for literate audiences. This is a natural reflection of the fact that our mission leaders are well-educated people who value books and literacy. However, Chiang and Lovejoy's book illustrates the fact that in order to connect with this vast segment of the global community, it is imperative that we adopt new understandings and methods to connect oral preference learners with the good news of Jesus Christ.

Beyond Literate Western Models tells the story, articulates its significance, and captures the state-of-the-art thinking on orality that was presented at the mini global consultation on orality and theological education hosted by the Billy Graham Center at Wheaton College. This resource will enable theological educators to catch up with a rapidly developing movement, and will provide them with the tools to help equip a new generation of pastors and mission leaders to respond to a new challenge of historic magnitude.

This book opens the window on a great new vista on world missions. It also opens the doorway to train and deploy great numbers of people who will be able to tell the Greatest Story in fresh and creative ways to those who have never heard. This is about as exciting and compelling as it gets in the great enterprise of world missions!

Billy Graham, John Stott, and the great leaders of their generation would have little experience in this field. However, I can imagine how pleased they would be with Chiang, Lovejoy, and their colleagues in the orality movement as they chart the course into this compelling new mission frontier.

This book does just that. It shows the way for us through the voices and perspectives of the world's leading orality missiologists. Samuel Chiang and Grant Lovejoy have brought together a remarkable team in selecting the most influential voices.

This is a book that will be prized by the Lausanne Movement and will be studied carefully by our leaders. It is one that will inform you and inspire you to action. I commend it to you. Read it carefully, then go back and read it again as you develop a plan. Then give it away so that the impact of this book is multiplied.

S. Douglas Birdsall, Honorary Chairman
The Lausanne Movement

President and CEO, American Bible Society

PROLOGUE

Samuel E. Chiang

The Back Story...

"We are seeing something happening in the theological arena. There are oral Bible schools popping up in many places. We have been praying for this for the last four years!" Ever since Linda Bemis, Prayer Director for the International Orality Network, told me those words over a Skype call, they have been etched indelibly into my mind. *How did I miss this?* I wondered. *How did I miss a developing trend? Was it time for a consultation? Where does one begin to propose an idea that will have credibility and influence?*

After much prayer, I went to Wheaton College to see Scott Moreau, long-time Editor of *Evangelical Missions Quarterly*, to propose an idea of a by-invitation-only consultation. He told me I was in the wrong place and needed to see Lon Allison, Executive Director of the Billy Graham Center. I was deflated. It was a snowy Friday afternoon in February, already 4:15 p.m., and I did not have an appointment. Ready to exit the building, I sensed I was to stay and visit Lon's office.

Always affable and kind, Lon not only received me for a visit, but listened carefully to the idea:

> *There are 5.7 billion oral preference learners in the world, and we are seeing oral Bible schools popping up in different parts of the world. This has implication for evangelism, church, and theological education. Should we consult together on this subject matter?*

After a couple of questions, he said, "Let's do it." I was delighted. Then he asked about the timing, possibly in the fall season when more students and faculty might benefit together? I sensed the event should be held in June. He looked at me quizzically as this was only four months away. Nevertheless, we decided to host the consultation at the end of June.

What was the theme and what were the questions? Will people come with such short notice? Who will present papers? After all, we did not wish for just a small handful of people to present papers; we desired a collective knowledge that would stimulate interaction. *Finally, what would be the consultation design format so as to create maximum synergy?*

We were off on a faith journey!

Cross Currents

Theological education has served the Church through sharpening students' intellects, training their wills, and forming their characters. Western theological education, influenced by the constraints of accreditation associations, has focused on intellectual formation, often to the neglect of the development of the whole person. Our education orientation often focuses on the "here and now," with a deficit attention to the long-term vision of educating the whole person for evangelism and discipleship, which leads to community and societal transformation. Western theological curricula have typically emphasized covering an extensive range of topics and progressively mastering difficult subjects. This has resulted in theological education for the educational elite and a lack of attention to the priesthood of ordinary believers.

Our cognitive approach has served the West, but the majority of the world and the Majority Church tend to approach education differently. In the majority of the world, the educational approach tends to focus on the development of the whole person, with intensity on knowing specific subject matters well. The Majority World tends to focus on process and is less product-driven. The majority of the world also has a greater proportion of oral (auditory) learners than that of visual learners, 60 compared to 40 percent, whereas it is reversed in Western societies.

Whereas the West tends to focus on a process of establishing principles, moving to guidelines, observing practices, and collecting stories, the majority of the world reverses the process and moves from stories to practices to guidelines to principles.

The biblical storytelling movement has discovered the enormous effectiveness of using storytelling in non-Western cultures, and with that, new trends in non-formal education have been popping up from Mombasa to Manila to Mumbai. Moreover, accredited theological education institutions have also started to recognize the importance of this trend in matters of andragogical (adult learning) consideration, curriculum, and granting of degrees in this field of study.

Reconceiving the Problem

We note the Bible is written, yet with a deliberate inclusion of the oral: God had Moses teach the people a poem so they could remember what he had done (a form of distribution of the scriptures via memorization); the biblical texts were composed for oral presentation as the Old and New Testaments were read aloud to large groups of people; renditions of the Psalms are accompanied with specific instruments. The New Testament world was both literate and oral, but over 90 percent of the population at that time could not read or write in the heart languages of the various peoples.

The seminal Lausanne Occasional Paper No. 54, published in 2005 as *Making Disciples of Oral Learners*, addressed how and why Christians should reach out to oral learners. The paper indicated that reading and writing are based upon oral communication, but "when literacy persists in a culture for generations, it begins to change the way people think, act, and communicate" so much so that literates cannot recognize oral style or how different it is from their own written style. They then try to evangelize oral communicators from their literate style. This makes understanding God's message very difficult for oral learners and communicators.

Often, we have said to classes of adult students to "contextualize" our theological classes into forms that can be used right away, but what if those are oral forms with specific cultural sounds, etc.? We often grade theological research papers based upon reference books. Is a community that is "doing" theology in real time through discussions not as valid? When global standards of biblical knowledge are diminishing, are there means to facilitate the whole-person learning process so as to increase biblical awareness? Are there means to affirm and empower oral learners so that they may be effective in evangelism and discipleship, which may lead to community and societal transformation?

After much prayer and careful consideration, the programming team for the consultation (Grant Lovejoy, Chuck Madinger, Mark Overstreet, Roland Moody, David Swarr, and I) decided the event should be called "Beyond Literate Western Models: Contextualizing Theological Education in Oral Contexts." This by-invitation-only consultation was to be global in nature, small in size, and case-study driven with mutual learning for potential implementation. We were delighted that the Billy Graham Center at Wheaton College saw the strategic nature of this consultation and agreed to host it in June 2012.

We recognized this was a *kairos* moment to bring together a small group of thought-leaders who are exploring non-formal theological education for oral learners, along with an innovative group of leaders in formal theological education who are pushing the boundaries of contextualizing Western theological education in oral contexts. This working consultation brought together innovators in theological education for oral contexts in order to analyze the challenges, present case studies of effective new approaches, and explore ways to collaborate for continued progress in this aspect of theological education.

Consultation Scope

The consultation intentionally focused on "Contextualizing Theological Education in Oral Contexts," where the oral communicators depend mostly upon spoken, non-print means to learn and communicate with others. Oral learners rely upon spoken language for communication, and their mental framework is oral rather than literate. Oral leaders have a preference for receiving, memorizing, and processing information in an oral format rather than print, and may come from oral traditions where bodies of knowledge are passed down orally from past generations. They, along with their communities and societies, may have an orature (oral literature) collection of hymns, proverbs, poetry, myths, dances, stories, and songs. Often, the orature is expressed in rhythm and repetition, with culturally-specific sounds and thematic settings.

We invited case studies for presentation, addressing questions (e.g., If leaders are readers, then, can non-readers be leaders?) We raised further questions (e.g., How do we affirm and empower leaders who are oral by nature to train others?) We were seeking to influence the development of this notable trend in theological education in oral contexts.

Imagine with us a horizontal plane in a circular room where the oral leader is in the center of the room, and imagine that the circular room is divided equally by four radii, resulting in four equal arcs of 90 degrees each. For our purposes, we shall call each equal arc a "Perspective." We were curious as to the *what and how* each Perspective interacted with and affected the oral leader. In conducting a horizontal 360 with the oral leader, we used four different Perspectives, each covering a 90 degree arc: formal institutional training and the oral leader, non-formal training and the oral leader, andragogy (adult learning) and the oral leader, and affirmation and empowering the oral leader.

In the working consultation, there were paper presentations and responses to each of the articles written within that Perspective, distilling, identifying, and analyzing challenges for oral learners from four different perspectives focusing on:

Formal Institutional and Degree Granting
a. What do we impart to learners about oral learners?
b. How do we help leaders to work with oral learners?
c. How do we make theological education more inclusive of oral learners?
d. How do we make theological education more beneficial to oral learners?

Non-formal Oral Training Programs or Courses
a. Why are the training programs popping up?
b. What do training program look like?

Andragogical Approaches among Adults

    a. How do adult oral preference learners learn?

    b. What are some case studies of how adult oral learners use different ways to reinforce learning?

Affirming and Empowering Oral Learners/Leaders and Their Approaches

    a. What are areas to unlearn and areas to (re)discover?

    b. What are means to create confidence with result orientation?

To encourage the thinking of all invitees, we asked ten additional questions:

1. What are your hopes and dreams for theological education in oral contexts into the future?
2. What expectations do you have for this consultation to modify your perspective on theological education on the field?
3. What led you to alter (or consider altering) your approach to theological education for oral cultures?
4. How has your understanding of revelation (God speaks to humanity) informed your view of accommodating oral culture learning preferences?
5. What changes have you and your ministry made in order to contextualize theological education for oral cultures?
6. What impact have you seen as a result of those changes?
7. Can you give us an example of someone who was affected by your efforts?
8. What advice would you give to others who are considering making similar changes?
9. What would you do differently if you had to do it over?
10. In what ways does scripture continue to shape and transform your work with oral learners?

Due to the short ramp-up time, the programming team requested experienced academicians and practitioners, representing both institutions and organizations from the Global South and North, to write 2,000-word papers which may cite major works. They described not only the "why and what" is being done, but also the "how" it was done. We have carefully edited the presentation for this book format so as to achieve layout format congruence.

Furthermore, we requested the authors propose questions to explore and challenges to consider, thus creating the DNA and the dynamic for the consultation process itself, and also for future conversations, debates, and research in this arena that affects education, church, training, missions, and resource allocation.

Many Joined in this Faith Journey

We sent out over 50 invitations; we were praying for 30 to attend. In the end, we had 42 academicians and practitioners, representing 18 institutions and 14 different organizations. This book and bonus items on the website represent our work together, and this is why we have included a short bio of each of the participants. The participants' voices were indispensable in shaping our collaborative learning, our "aha" moments, and our future actions.

This book is divided into four sections, with each section representing a 90-degree Perspective. The chapters within each of the Perspectives represent each practitioner's excellent, thoughtful, and reflective presentation, his or her own voice through the chapter, and his or her dialogue conversations throughout the consultation. At the end of each Perspective there is a respondent to the articles (chapters in this book) which synthesizes the Perspective, makes observations of strengths and weakness, and further questions to consider. All these heightened our "Imagineering" and sharpened our focus towards actionable outcomes. The Epilogue, written by Grant Lovejoy, represents both the dynamics from the format (the environment as we dived into the discussions and formulated action plans) and the actual initiatives that are flowing forth from the consultation. The Annotated Bibliography is the combined work of several contributors; we believe the inclusion of this section will provide you with greater ease to launch into the topic of orality and theological education.

Often, we lament what is on the cutting floor and left out of the book. We see it differently. In fact, there are bonus documents, videos, and interviews on the website. If you wish to download the chapters individually, or to view short video clips, including interviews, please use the URL address: *www.orality.net/ResourcesBillyGrahamCenter ConsultationOralityandTheologicalEducation or the QR Code on the bottom of this page, which will take you to the website section for both video interviews and other downloads.*

We invite you to join us in this journey of reflection, discussion, and collaboration...**to the Edge of Possibilities**...

PERSPECTIVE I:

Formal Education—Training Institutions and the Oral Preference Learner

As we moved into this mini-global consultation, we created expectations, and we wanted to meet them. The most oft-repeated expectations were: integration, building relationships, learning, listening, soaking, collaborating.

Participants asked if the theological education accreditation body should generate another structure for accrediting orality, and wondered if orality could be perceived as a threat to the "establishment". There were genuine reflections upon the possible need to re-examine our systems and methodologies, and ask what is essential and how it can be done in an oral fashion.

From the chapters in this section, we will be challenged with:

What is the role of contextualization with scripture and the world of cultures?

How do we handle the dialectical tensions?

Is the role of the teacher changing to become facilitator or validator?

Where is our starting point, and what is the role of accreditation?

How can we possibly have faculty and staff integration?

Each question has an impact on the learning process, the person and role of the educator, and how to function within the structure of the institution. What are your expectations, and will you consider reading through this section with a small group of colleagues and friends?

Chapter 1

How Should a Theological Institution Prepare Students/Leaders Who Will Go Out into the Field to Train Local People (Storytellers) to Tell Bible Stories Effectively?

Damon So

Introduction

The usefulness of the oral story approach in mission was clearly attested by the result of the approach reported in the Lausanne Cape Town meeting in 2010. There, I saw, via podcast, Samuel Chiang convening a session on this very significant approach that has been fruitfully employed in mission fields where the literacy level is low. The encouraging fruit of this approach raises the need for (1) greater reflection and understanding of what it is, and (2) the subsequent improvement and widening in the employment of this approach in mission.

It is the purpose of this brief paper to discuss these two aspects in the context of seminary training, where it is envisaged that students will be trained to go out to the mission field, where they will in turn train local storytellers to retell the stories of the Bible in local cultural forms.

The Oral Story Approach in the Bible and in Mission

Much of the Bible was written in the genre of narrative or story (e.g., the historical books in the Old Testament, and the Gospels and

Acts in the New Testament). It is almost certain that the initial forms of these narratives existed as oral stories that were later committed to writing and thus set in textual form.

In the last ten years, the oral aspect of the four canonical Gospels has been studied in the discipline of New Testament Studies with increasing intensity. Rather than seeing the Gospels as texts read by Christians and seekers privately in the first century, New Testament scholars have recovered the important fact that the texts were orally read or performed to a gathering of the local community of believers (and seekers), most of whom were not literate.

It is almost certain that when the writers edited and wrote the Gospel texts, they were aware how the texts would be used (i.e., orally performed). They would have written or edited the texts in a way amenable to oral performance, or the texts were written in such a way that their desired impact would be realized if the texts were read orally to a gathering of people. The same most probably applies to the Old Testament narratives. Thus, for the narratives in the Bible, there are two oral aspects—the oral form prior to being written down in text, and the oral performance based upon the written text.

Form and Content

The point made above serves to highlight the original oral nature of biblical narratives. The use of the oral story approach in contemporary mission is nothing more than recovering the original manner in which these narratives were recited to the audience. As the nature of biblical narratives is not a simplistic one, we should be reminded that the use of the oral story approach in contemporary mission should also not be simplistic, but should explore different nuances of such an approach for it to be fully effective.

For example, biblical stories were often told with a select audience in mind. Matthew, the most Jewish of the four Gospels, was first written and orally delivered to a predominantly Jewish audience.

In contrast, Luke was written and orally delivered to a predominantly Gentile audience. One may say that the same gospel message (the *content*) was written and orally delivered in slightly different *forms* for the sake of reaching different target audiences.

The relationship between form and content is a very important one for our contemporary mission in the world for the following reason: different people groups live in different cultures with different languages, with distinctive characteristics. An undesirable potential effect of globalization is that the unique characteristics of a culture may be eroded by a foreign imposing monoculture. This can also happen to missions where the Church in one context/culture is literally transplanted into another context/culture with no cultural sensitivities. This can cause unnecessary hindrance to the extension of God's kingdom into the local culture since a wholly foreign (and thus unfamiliar) culture is being brought together with the gospel to the local people. For culturally-sensitive missions, the messenger of the gospel needs to clothe the *content* of the true gospel in the local cultural *form*.

An important cultural form is that of storytelling, which exists in many developing countries where the people live together in a more communal manner than in the West, and their communal gathering is the context in which folk stories are told. (When I was little, I lived in such a context in a rural village in Hong Kong.) Other than the cultural form where stories are told by only one storyteller (which may be a profession in itself as in many parts of China), there are other cultural forms in which traditional stories are told or performed by a group of amateur or professional people (e.g., plays or operas with accompanying music and musicians for singing).

The Cantonese opera and Peking opera are two examples among a plethora of such popular folk performances in China. Some Chinese believers who are professional opera performers/singers have put Christian lyrics into well-known traditional Cantonese opera music, which is especially welcomed by the older generation. However, one has yet to see a full-blown opera performance of some biblical narrative that could have a significant impact on the Chinese mission field. Apart from these scant examples, as far as we know there is no intentional move to retell biblical stories in local Chinese cultural forms. (Note: The Oxford Centre for Mission Studies has a Chinese student researching these Chinese cultural *forms* of performance for transmitting the *content* of the Christian gospel. See section about seminary training.)

Story and Interpretation

Apart from the form of storytelling, one must not neglect the content of the Christian gospel being carried by the form. It is presumed that the content comes from the collection of stories we have in the Bible. Just as biblical stories are already interpreted stories, the stories we tell in a mission context carry the interpretations of the storytellers or those who train the storytellers (or the interpretation is given after the performance of the story).

Even biblical stories can be misinterpreted and orally presented to yield heretical ideas (e.g., Jesus Christ is merely divine or merely human; Jesus Christ is the only person in the Godhead [or the Father or the Spirit as the only divine person]; the gospel is merely about the future life to come and nothing in the present life and so engagement in the society or in the world is kept to a minimum). In view of the challenge of interpretation, biblical stories need be told from a biblically-sound perspective. This involves careful understanding of Christian doctrines/theology developed through centuries past.

Seminary Training

Because of the blessed fruit of the oral story approach in mission, the improvement and widening in the employment of this approach in mission are necessary in seminary and other forms of training. For the purpose of this paper, it is envisaged that seminary students will be trained to go out to the mission field, where they will train local storytellers to retell the stories of the Bible in local cultural forms with interpretation that is biblically sound.

The Oral Nature of the Biblical Narratives

Seminary students need to be made aware of the oral nature of biblical narratives, as briefly presented above. There have been many recent books on this topic. One example is James A. Maxey's *From Orality to Orality: A New Paradigm for Contextual Translation of the Bible*, which talks about contextualization, orality, and performance.

Diverse Cultural Forms and One Gospel Content

Students need to be made aware of the important relationship between the different cultural *forms* that can express the one *content* of the Christian gospel. This is a question of unity and diversity and could be foundationally treated from the Trinitarian perspective (the plurality of the Father, Son, and Holy Spirit in perfect dynamic unity). Regarding *form*, they should be aware of the need to work with local people in the field to look for different suitable cultural forms for presenting biblical stories that can involve one person or a group of people.

The Whole Gospel Story of Jesus

Regarding the *content* of the Christian gospel, the gospel story of Jesus occupies the pre-eminent place, but students should be instructed to avoid majoring on one phase of Jesus' earthly life only, as often seen in Western preaching. Often, liberal churches in the West major on the life of Jesus, while conservative churches often major on the death of Jesus, both without telling the full story of Jesus. This dichotomy between majoring on the life and majoring on the death of Jesus closely corresponds to the general dichotomy in mission between "social action only" and "proclamation only," neither of which grasp the full gospel story of Jesus and thereby do not practice the holistic gospel in mission.

By presenting the more complete story of Jesus in his birth, baptism, temptations, public ministry, entry into Jerusalem, death, resurrection, and universal reign, the oral story approach employed in non-Western contexts has presented a more holistic picture of Jesus Christ who thus *in the power of his person* has drawn many people unto himself. The success of the oral story approach is partly due to its accessible *form*. But this is not the only factor, because in adopting the story *form* (instead of a purely propositional or formulaic approach often found in the West), the more complete *content* of the story of Jesus is also presented which can account significantly for the fruit of this oral approach.

Indeed, it is the coming together of the *form* of the biblical story approach and the *content* associated with this approach that God has used to bring many people to himself. Seminary students need to be made aware of why God has used this approach. They need to learn about the historical background in Western Christianity concerning the Life of Jesus movement of the nineteenth-century liberal Protestants (which can be traced back to F. Schleiermacher) and the Reformation legacy in the conservatives.

Students need to learn that the oral story approach has cut one of the Gordian knots in divergent Western theologies and Christian traditions (between liberals and conservatives), albeit inadvertently. The other Gordian knot to be cut by the oral story approach is the divergence between biblical studies and systematic theology in Western academy.

Oral Storytelling Uniting Biblical Studies and Systematic Theology

The above divergence in Western theologies has already indicated that the underlying theologies could influence the way one interprets the story of Jesus or emphasizes only one part of that story. The story in the Bible remains the same for liberals and conservatives, but it has been interpreted in different ways, based upon different theologies.

This opens up the question of the relationship between systematic theology and biblical studies. Oral storytelling is not separated from training in biblical studies and systematic theology in the seminary and has the potential for uniting them for the following reason: For oral storytelling to be faithful to biblical revelation, students must learn sound theology that is biblical, since such theology will undergird the way they will interpret the story and teach others to retell the story in other forms. But to learn theology that is truly biblical, students have to learn to do their foundational homework in biblical studies, which will inform their interpretation of the story. They must learn to develop a biblical systematic theology *from* their biblical studies.

However, in the Western academy, biblical studies and systematic theology are separate departments with the result that (1) the systematic theology being taught may not be truly biblical and (2) biblical interpretation does not result in concrete systematized theology. However, oral storytelling calls for sound biblical interpretation that is developed into sound theology that is truly biblical and used to interpret the story.

Instead of seeing oral storytelling as a third separate department in seminary, it should be seen as the department which brings together the two major departments in seminary education. But this will call for significant changes in the way these two departments operate, especially in breaking down the often very strict partition between the two (see So 2006).

A student thus trained in all three departments will have the necessary knowledge to guide and train local storytellers to tell biblical stories with great faithfulness and power. This point pertains to the content of the story being told. To present faithfully the content of biblical stories, three kinds of interpretation are necessary:

- Interpretations in biblical studies
- Development of these biblical studies interpretations into systematic theology, which is a second-order interpretation (i.e., interpretation of biblical studies interpretations)
- Interpreting biblical stories in oral storytelling using the knowledge in (1) and (2).

Hence, oral storytelling calls for the coming together of biblical studies and systematic theology and can help break the rigid divide between the two in Western seminaries and academy. (Note: Preaching has a similar function, but is not the same as oral storytelling [e.g., preaching can be merely propositional in nature and therefore needs not draw interpretation of stories and theology together in the way described above].)

To illustrate the three kinds of interpretation involved in oral storytelling, one can look at telling the gospel story of Jesus. First, passages covering every phase in the gospel story of Jesus (including his birth, public ministry, death, resurrection, and universal reign) need to be studied carefully with reference to the literary and historical background. Second, a biblical theology is developed from such biblical studies to understand who Jesus is in relation to his Father and the Holy Spirit, and the significance of his work (i.e., a theology of the Trinity is developed from sound biblical interpretation). Third, the story of Jesus is retold from the perspective of his foundational relationship with his Father through the Spirit, avoiding the mistake of Unitarianism, Modalism, Tritheism, or other heretical interpretations, thus presenting Jesus faithfully as he is presented in the Bible (see So 2010).

Other Issues for Discussion

1. Skills of performance: rhetoric, aesthetics, poetic, etc.
2. Spirituality of trainers and storytellers
   - Understanding and interpreting the stories in the Bible with the guidance of the Holy Spirit
   - Delivering the stories, using the local form, in the power and guidance of the Holy Spirit, possibly involving many believers working in the unity of the Spirit
   - Spiritual formation of the trainer and storytellers, prayer and dependence upon the Holy Spirit
3. Fellowship of trainers and performers/storytellers
4. Humility and incarnational approach in training local leaders; willingness of the trainer to learn and delegate

5. Project: Seminary students in groups employing an oral storytelling approach to sharing the gospel with people close to the seminary, but in a different sub-culture, using their cultural form and language

6. Case studies on the use of the oral storytelling approach in mission: positive or negative cases/points for critical study

7. Learning cycle: preparation, performance, evaluation, revised preparation, revised performance, further evaluation, etc.

8. The role of explicit interpretation after the storytelling: preaching

9. Media, radio, TV

10. Provision or equipping of teachers in seminaries for training students who will in turn train local storytellers.

Application in the West: Using the fuller story of Jesus as given in the Gospels has cut one of the Gordian knots in mission (i.e., by presenting a fuller picture of Jesus to the audience). This very point has great implication for missions in the West. People in the West also like stories (e.g., in films, televisions, novels, etc.), but something in the history of the Western Church and its theological education/training has produced ministers and pastors who often think and preach propositionally, therefore majoring on the Epistles in the New Testament (there are historical reasons for this).

The result is that in many pulpits in the West the story of Jesus has been neglected, and even in evangelism/missions, the same pattern of propositional dominance persists. That is why the oral approach utilizing the gospel story of Jesus is such a breath of fresh air. The story of Jesus can make the same powerful impact on the audience in the West as in the non-West. The success of the oral approach in non-Western context is due not only to its *form* (oral), but also to its *content* (story of Jesus). The right form and content work together very well in non-Western contexts, and I believe the same can be true in Western contexts.

Chapter 2

Africa Theological Seminary

Phil Walker

Africa Theological Seminary (ATS) came into existence at the request of pastors and Christian leaders in the northwestern part of Kenya. Many of these leaders had attended post-secondary diploma programs but wanted to advance their education to the next level. They also wanted to remain in the ministry, but this precluded full-time residential study. With this criteria and philosophy, ATS was launched in 1992 with the following parameters:

- Discipleship/transformation had to be central to the curriculum and structure
- All programs of study had to be validated by existing accrediting groups
- ATS would be founded upon an in-service model with learners coming for five weeks, three times a year

With these parameters in place, ATS developed a partnership with Global University (a fully accredited Christian university in the Pentecostal tradition, based out of Springfield, Missouri, USA).

Graduates received a joint degree from Global University and Africa Theological Seminary. More recently, ATS has been going through the accreditation process with the Accrediting Council for Theological Education in Africa (ACTEA). It has also applied for a charter from the Commission for Higher Education in Kenya.

These groups require that we maintain a certain traditional approach even as we have sought new ways to bring about the goals of the seminary. Those goals include a focus on five key areas of a leader's life: core beliefs, character, commitments, competencies, and capacity. Measures of success are demonstrated by the transformation in the leaders and in the community impact they make in returning to their congregations.

Theological Education and Orality

The orality movement has surfaced some critical issues for theological education. Over the past 30 years, education has made amazing strides in methodology. Many of these are in relationship to the way learning takes place. Whether we are talking about Malcolm Knowles or Howard Gardner, the focus has been on how people process information and learn. Orality is another step in this process. It would be a serious mistake to think of orality simply as a means for reaching non-literate, oral societies. Orality has surfaced three key points that theological education must consider and apply to its methods and programs:

1. Primary oral learners must have a non-print way to plant churches and grow disciples. We see this being addressed by churches and mission agencies.
2. Secondary oral learners (Ong 32) make up the vast majority of our staff, faculty and target audience. Also, many of these come from primary oral learning congregations. Systemic changes need to be made in the way we educate and we train our learners to train others.
3. Finally, we need to understand that recent research has shown

that most behavior has its roots in the unconscious brain. The primal brain does not learn systematically but processes all information through a "belief" grid and then incorporates the new data into the "story" of the individual, providing the brain with schema that guides behavior. Traditional literate approaches to education have little impact on this unconscious schema as the unconscious cannot directly process information presented in the traditional literate style. Virtues and values must be expressed behaviorally if they are to become part of who we are. The degree of impact on our character is directly proportional to following four actions: Focus, Feedback, Intensity and Time (FFIT). It is interesting to note that stories provide a vicarious experience that directly impacts our unconscious schema, which in turn impacts our behavior. In effect, those stories told with the greatest intensity and focus, over the longest period of time, reinforced with reward/punishment (feedback), have the greatest impact on life choices and character.

ATS Application of Orality

ATS is beginning to apply our new knowledge in two major areas:

1. Ensuring system-wide participation and support from our staff and faculty
2. Starting to change key areas of our program

Staff and Faculty

We had our first orality training with our key international leaders in Johannesburg, South Africa. Leaders from different countries joined together for training with Samuel Chiang and Bramuel Musya. In April 2012, a number of our key faculty attended the International Orality Network launch in Nairobi, Kenya. In June, select staff attended the ION Consultation in Wheaton, Illinois. In September 2012, U.S. staff and board members attended the international ION conference in Denver, Colorado.

At the end of September 2012, we hosted our own orality conference for staff, faculty, alumni, and interested parties on the Kitale campus. We have already made books and materials on orality available to staff and faculty at the seminary and have asked them to read the materials.

Program Impact
Orality will impact us in three key areas:

1. Relationship to primary oral learners
2. Relationship to secondary oral learners
3. Impact on character and transformation of learners

Relationship to Primary Oral Learners

Training programs: ATS is situated in the northwestern part of Kenya, where a number of nomadic and semi-nomadic tribes reside. We are also closely tied to a group (Sabaot) which until recently was classified as an unreached people group (less than 10 percent Christian). The majority of these groups can be classified as primary oral learners or recent secondary oral learners. In the case of the Sabaot, we have a training center in their area. Secondary oral learners work at the certificate level (primary schooling) and secondary level (secondary and post-secondary diplomas). Historically, ATS has used traditional literate materials to develop programs to train leaders. However, we are now working with Musya (ION East Africa) to incorporate his three-year training program. This approach opens the door to provide training for leaders who will be planting churches among primary oral learners.

Training the trainer: In addition to using the orality methods to work directly with leaders in a certificate program, we see the need and urgency to train our learners at every level on the unique learning style of oral learning. We are developing classes that focus on oral-literate learning styles (Jim Slack Learning Grid, Earl A. Bowen and Dorothy N. Bowen 1988). Using Slack's five learning styles as the basis, we are able to focus on the various "best practices" for communicating to different groups.

Relationship to Secondary Oral Learners

The majority of our learners, faculty, and staff can be classified as secondary oral learners (Ong 1982). If there is a correlation between oral learning styles and field-dependent learners then we could say, based on Earl A. Bowen and Dorothy N. Bowen (1988), 91 percent of learners in Africa, even post-secondary learners, are secondary oral learners.

While we have sought to incorporate andragogical methods in our training, we need to go much further. We are appreciative of researchers and past writers like Malcolm Knowles (1984), Bowen and Bowen (1988), Walter Ong, and Howard Gardner (1995). But we cannot stop with their fine work. In our theological educational institutions we must find better ways to communicate and train our learners to communicate more effectively. Ralph Winter made the statement: "To the degree we successfully export our current model of theological education to where the church is growing the fastest will be to the degree to which we slow church growth" (ACCESS conference 1988). I believe we are in the position now to move beyond rhetoric to application of teaching methods that teach the mind *and* train the heart.

We are in the early stages of planning our changes. While our faculty and staff have been considering how to adjust their own teaching methods, we have not instituted any sweeping changes in our curriculum yet. The following are some of the things we are doing and/or anticipate doing.

Developing instructor evaluations that include teaching methods which align with that of secondary oral learners. Because of their advanced degrees and need for constant study, our entire faculty are at least at the far end of the secondary oral learner scale, if not into literate learners. This presents a challenge to our institutions. "What was good enough for me should be good enough for them" has to change. Staff and faculty training will begin focusing on understanding and applying oral learning strategies.

From the very beginning of ATS in 1992 we **used a model of training called** *synergogy* (Mouton and Blake 1985). It is advertised as a blended model between andragogy and pedagogy. We found the test-taking model to be very powerful in building team interaction. We will expand this to use other options listed in the book that fit into the secondary oral learning model. Internet-based research will provide ample information about this approach.

At present, we are **evaluating specific courses** which could be developed that would introduce the theory and the methods of orality. We want our learners to have the skill set necessary to identify their audience in relationship to the orality grid (see www.storyrunners. com/orality/how-oral-learners-communicate). We will do this through a stand-alone course and reinforce it by what we do throughout the seminary in the teaching of other courses. We are convinced modeling is one of the keys to learning (Bandura 2007). This also means a constant reinforcement with our faculty with regards to their teaching methods.

Recently, the seminary has **entered into partnerships** that will impact the campus and learners. In addition to being part of ION East Africa, the seminary has entered into a partnership with Davar, a provider of materials for oral learners. We desire to become a hub for materials and techniques that learners can use to reach into the oral community with the gospel.

ATS **requires learners to put into practice what they learn**. This is done by requiring that 20 percent of every course grade be from application between terms. We also require that ten credit hours be earned through field projects. We are in the process of aligning both to oral methods.

Finally, we need to move beyond the issues of orality to understand that the use of stories and many of the methods we are advocating are not limited to a learning style. These early means of learning, stories, poems, songs, dance, and plays have been used for centuries to pass on community, virtues, and values. Rather than jettison them as the "old" way, we need to incorporate them as the foundation of theological education. Therefore, we desire to **build a culture at ATS that uses these various means to pass on the very core beliefs, virtues, and values that define us as disciples of Jesus**.

Impact on Character and Transformation of Learners

Our research and study over the past five years has focused on how God has designed us to learn to become more like Jesus (2 Cor. 3:28; Rom. 8:29). Our concern has been that ATS has moved too far down the academic path without due concern for our core desire to make disciples. We have looked at past models (Cannell 2006, 126), current practice, and most importantly, the latest research on how people learn. Our primary focus has been on character development, specifically how people become more like Jesus.

While writers like Dallas Willard (1991), Richard Foster (1993) and John Coe (2001) have been helpful, they have not provided a good understanding of the mechanisms that form character. That has led to the study of the unconscious and its systemic search for order. Transformation is the process of inculcating the story of God as found in his word. We do this by living out the word and by rehearsing God's word through stories, song, and drama. By constantly rehearsing God's word in such ways, the Holy Spirit transforms our personal story to fit into his story.

We believe that many of the principles of oral learning apply to this very goal. Character transformation is about Focus, Feedback, Intensity, and Time (FFIT) empowered by the Holy Spirit. Our goal in theological education is to provide the right focus in order to produce godly character. The more you incorporate the story of God into your life, the more your life reflects the story of God. Simply put, where your focus is, your heart follows. To put it another way, as Jesus said, "Wherever your treasure is, there the desires of your heart will also be" (Matt. 6:21).

At ATS, we are working on realigning both our course and our very culture. This is achieved in a number of ways.

- Building devotions around biblical stories. We have obtained Story Through the Bible from our partner, Walk Thru the Bible. Every learner coming in for his or her term will be given this book and asked to use it for devotions. He or she will read and meditate on an assigned story as his or her devotion.
- During chapel, we will use the same story from which to teach. This will be presented orally and then the speaker will draw lessons from the material.
- We have in place accountability groups. These groups will use their time together to review the story and share with the group what God is saying to them in their devotions. They will also be challenged to share the story with one another without the aid of their books.
- We will notify all instructors of what story the learners are reading and ask them, when possible, to include the story in their lesson plans.
- We will encourage the physical practice of living out the virtues in daily life. For example, from the beginning, we started the practice of cleaning dishes after a meal. Everyone, including faculty and staff, took part. This practice became a hallmark of the seminary. It was reinforced by the giving of a towel at graduation to signify servanthood. It has been expanded as classes have begun to adopt community service projects. These team and community activities reinforce the process of transformation.
- As an institution, we will identify one or two virtues that will become the focus during each term. The goal is to identify how to reinforce these virtues through multiple ways. Our goal is to narrow our focus and increase intensity to produce greater change.
- Finally, we will seek to introduce more stories and biographies that reinforce the transformational process in our assignments.

Conclusion

We believe Africa is at the beginning of its golden age. Prosperity will expand educational options and increase the skills and capacity of the African workforce. We also believe that by reaching back to the power of oral learning that was prevalent just a few years ago, we can rediscover the keys that will help unlock personal transformation.

African theological education has the potential to break out of the mold of a Western system built upon the faulty foundation of a purely literate style of education, and introduce the world to a model of theological education that has the right blend of literacy and character emphasis and methods. We must make this a focus in the days ahead.

I do, however, have one very strong warning. I watched and participated in the introduction and expansion of Theological Education by Extension (TEE) in Africa. In the early days we used the programmed instruction materials (Text Africa) developed for TEE Africa (Fred and Grace Holland).

While it never caught on in the way Ralph Winter had hoped, it did play a part in training secondary oral learners without access to traditional schools. However, it failed on two accounts: (1) it was seen as the method to be used by those who did not have enough education to go to "real" schools, and (2) the curriculum became identified with the model. To this day, many people will tell you that programmed texts and TEE are synonymous.

Winter wrote that any use of TEE should begin at the highest educational level to ensure diffusion to all levels. It does not work the other way around. We, in the orality movement, are at a crossroads. If theological institutions cannot or will not provide the credibility and the validity of the model, then it will remain a phenomenon used by missionaries and others working in societies made up of primary oral learners. We, in the formal theological educational arena, have the power and the ability to provide the credibility that will take the movement from periphery to the center of discipleship. But we must act now to draw the model into the essence of our training.

Chapter 3

Oral Bible Story Telling Training at New India Bible Seminary, Kerala, India

Mary Verghese

Translate to Transform

"In the beginning was the Word and the Word was with God and the Word was God" (John 1:1). "God spoke the world into being out of nothing" (Gen. 1). The spoken word *transformed* nothingness into our beautiful earth. God *transformed* the soil of the earth into a live human being in his image and by his breath.

A word of instruction given to the first couple by God was *mistranslated* by Satan, giving it a different meaning: "No, you will not surely die—but you will become like God (Gen. 3:4). The impact of that *mistranslation* was disobedience, resulting in the *transformation* of humans from the image of God to the image of Satan, a process that sadly still continues. The DNA of human beings has changed forever.

"Then the Word became flesh and dwelt among us" (John 1:3); the Word (Jesus) was *transformed* into a human being to dwell among us and changed the direction of *transformation* through his death and resurrection. He left instructions to follow if we want to be *transformed* back into the image of God and the earth to be *transformed* into God's kingdom. "Your Kingdom come—on earth as it is in Heaven" (Matt. 6:10). The responsibility is entrusted to all Christ's disciples to teach and make disciples of all nations and languages in order to *transform* this world into the nature of his kingdom. The word, that is the scripture, is to be *translated* and presented in a language understandable for effective *transformation* in the right direction, which means *transformation* back into the original nature and in the image of God. We are to *translate* it without changing its meaning like Satan did.

Orality and Oral Bible Story Telling in the Indian Context

It is a known fact that 2/3 (70 percent) of the world's population are oral learners. In India, the number of oral learners is of a much higher percentage, as there are a large number of people even among the literate group who cannot read or write with comprehension. Besides, there are at least 110 languages in India that are oral in nature and are Bible-less. They too need the word of God in order to be *transformed* to the nature and image of God. Evangelists often present the gospel in a language that is not close to people's hearts, interpreted in the preacher's frame of mind, rather than that of the listeners. This makes it difficult for them to identify with what is being preached. As a result, it is easily forgotten. In effect, these are seeds sown in the by-ways.

India's constitution guarantees freedom to practice and propagate one's own religion. But we come across incidents that indicate that we may not be able to enjoy that freedom for long. Christians are being falsely accused of forceful conversion, which is against the law in some states of India now. Occasionally, the demonstrative aspects of the gospel are being misinterpreted as bribing for conversion. The possibility of the Bible in printed form being restricted or banned in the future cannot be denied. That is when the stories, songs, dramas, folklores, poems, proverbs, etc., presented in oral forms, repeated and learned and shared, will become useful since they can be handed down to generations by oral repetition.

Hence, there is an urgency in getting scripture out in the oral story format. In addition, this is the method used by the "Master Teacher." The method that is SIMPLE (Scarborough 2009, 47).

S	Stories and parables
I	Interactive
M	Multi-track, reaching people in multiple levels
P	Preparation
L	Love: the passion and motivation provides foundation for integrity
E	Action and results-oriented

New India Evangelistic Association and Its Passion in Oral Bible Storying (OBS)

New India Evangelistic Association (NIEA) envisions a NEW INDIA, an India *transformed* for Christ. The director board of NIEA is committed to holistic *transformation* of individuals. Hence, it has a multifaceted strategy, evolved on the basis of evidenced needs.

Felt needs for flood victims in Bihar in 2008 gave the NIEA more emphasis on orality and OBS. NIEA has completed 25 Bible stories and related dramas and songs in six Bihar languages and distributed them through Proclaimers and audio Bibles in partnership with The Seed Company, T4 Global, and Davar Partners. We are seeing the result through rapidly multiplying churches in the Bible-less language groups of Bihar. Bihar State Network of Language and Church Planting Initiative now facilitates networking among various church-planting agencies as a results-based management of translation and church planting.

Last Commandment Initiative and NIEA

Last Commandment Initiative (LCI) is formed as a network of church planters, linguistic and translation agencies, and resourcing partners such as The Seed Company, with the aim to provide God's word to the entire Bible-less language communities in India.

NIEA Director Dr. Alex Philip has had direct involvement in its formation and functioning. LCI has a mandate of starting translation in all 110 Bibles-less languages by 2025. LCI also plans to provide community development and teaching material for *transform*ing the community.

For practical purposes, the country is divided into seven zones. NIEA is the lead administrative agency for the central zone and the Bihar model is replicated there. In the central zone, Bible storying is being done by mother tongue translators coached by consultants in training, and supervised and guided by linguistic and translation experts.

There is a great need for mother tongue translators and coaches from within India in large numbers to achieve the LCI mandate. This awareness led to a proposal for a training program affiliated with a theological training institution so that there will be a pool of coaches available. At the same time, the theologically-literate community will be made aware of the need and possibilities in this area and can explore various ways of using OBS in the mission field and integrating OBS in theological training.

Orality Training in New India Bible Seminary

New India Bible Seminary (NIBS) is the training institution contributing to the *transform*ative vision of NIEA by training leaders for the mission field. "At NIBS, the training ethos has been to prepare graduates for the context of the future mission by providing tailor-made responsive training modules," says Dr. Jessy Jason. NIBS's curriculum is based upon The Context Based *Transform*ative learning model coined by Dr. Jason Thomas, the Principal. The seminary training is closely associated with the churches represented by the student community.

At present, there are about 200 students representing 21 states and five neighboring countries enrolled in formal theological training programs: BTh (three years), MDiv (two years), and MTh in

Holistic Child Development (two years). The basic entry requirement is completion of higher secondary education.

The seminary was established in 1975, and since then it has shown continuous growth. The seminary faculty is committed to academic, character, spiritual, and mission formation of its students. The student population is multicultural, multiethnic, interdenominational, and mission-oriented. NIBS provides a good ground for introducing orality training.

As an initial step of loosening the soil, a two-week orientation Seminar in Oral Bible Story Telling (OBST) was conducted at NIBS by specialists in OBST for students in June 2011. There were 65 participants. Almost all the students expressed that OBST was helpful for their own personal study of the Bible; they felt that OBST was a good method of teaching the Bible to the illiterate, as well as the literate. One of the students commended, "We love this method, as this gives wide-ranging possibilities for bridge-building to the unreached people groups and interestingly without barriers of age or educational status or religious background."

As an outcome of this workshop, Bible Storying Clubs were formed on campus and they met on a regular basis for prayer and Bible study. A few of the students wanted to have in-depth experience in OBST in order to make a career of it. Seven of the ten students registered for graduate OBST Training were from this group. It became evident that integrating OBST to the theologically literate would result in "getting it right" and "getting it across" for effective *transformation*.

Today at NIBS, two types of programs are in the planning and implementation stage, with NIEA/NIBS/TSC partnering together.

Orientation Course in Oral Bible Storytelling
Desired outcomes:

- All students will be introduced to orality and its importance to ministry opportunities in India.
- All students will be provided with an oral strategy (OBS) to use in the ministry in future.
- All students will be encouraged to look at a full-time career with involvement in OBS projects as facilitators or other key roles.

Impact:

1. Students will develop:
   a. An appreciation of OBST as a mission strategy
   b. Beginning skills in OBST
2. Internalization and acceptance of OBST among faculty
3. NIBS owning, coordinating, and running the program
4. Integration of OBST into the already-accredited BTh program
5. Students visualize OBST as their long-term ministerial career in India

Design:

For two weeks twice a year, OBST orientation training will be conducted by experts on the field for all the students at NIBS: one in July 2012 and another in October 2012. These will be scheduled in the regular timetable of the seminary. The vision is to have a department of orality in the seminary with faculty prepared, adequate infrastructure, learning resources made available, and orality integrated as a module of study in the accredited BTh program.

NIBS Graduate Student OBS Facilitator Training Program

This program is designed for training the graduates from NIBS and other seminaries in India to become OBS facilitators so there will be a pool of OBS facilitators available to meet the Last Commandment execution plan. The curriculum will include academic and on-the-job training in the field.

Expected Outcome

- The students will be equipped to lead or play a significant role in OBST projects in Bible-less language groups in India, positioning the students to be part of the LCI execution plan to reach the remaining 110+ languages without scripture in India.
- Many of these students will become trainers of others to be OBS workshop facilitators.

Candidate Selection Criteria

1. Basic Bible training (BTh or MDiv)
2. Competency/fluency in the language of wider culture where Bible-less languages are represented
3. Competency in English
4. Willingness to be accountable to the technical body that supervises the work
5. Clear understanding of the vision of LCI
6. Compliance to the statement of faith
7. Commitment to remain in Bible translation work for long-term ministry

The curriculum includes preliminary theory course for four months. During the rest of the year, students will have at least three additional workshops where skills are provided in OBST, crafting of stories, formation of Storying Fellowship Groups, etc.

During workshops, all candidates are assigned work experience with translation teams on the field in the appropriate language community. Generally, training in the field will be done in the language of wider communication spoken by the candidate and where Bible-less minority languages exist in proximity.

For example, Manipuri candidates will be sent to Manipur state to train with teams doing translation work in any of the language projects in the geographical area of Manipur. Their skills will be developed in the language of wider communication, and eventually they will be able to lead multiple Storying Teams (in multiple Bible-less languages) which are in close proximity to this particular language of wider communication.

Preliminary Theory Courses

Cross-cultural Training	2 weeks
Orality	1week
Scripture Translation Principles	1 week
Ethnomusicology	2 days
Workshop on Oral Bible Storytelling	2 weeks
Computer and Keyboarding Training	(individual needs based)
Additional Workshops (three more)	6 weeks

Placement for Supervised Work Experience

Students will be assigned to the field for supervised production-based experience according to their linguistic background. They will be paid a stipend. The work experience will be interspaced with four two-week workshops per year.

(Note: The first batch of candidates has been selected and classes started in April 2012. A coordinator has been appointed by NIBS to manage the programs.)

Challenges

1. Recruiting appropriate students who will be committed for long-term involvement
2. Availability of personal and material learning resources
3. Development of indigenous faculty
4. Selecting appropriate placement of the students for work experience
5. Availability of appropriate candidates from the underdeveloped mother tongue areas
6. Spiritual mentoring of the students while they are away from the center

7. Obtaining cooperation from the local theologically-literate community
8. Challenges related to partnership

"This Gospel of the Kingdom will be preached in the whole world as a testimony to all nations, and then the end will come" (Matt. 24:14). Let us be vigilant and use our time, talent, and treasure to quicken the day.

Chapter 4
A Response to the Articles in Perspective I

Emmanuel Chemengich

Introduction

As I respond to three papers by Damon So, Phil Walker, and Mary Verghese, it is worth noting the two contexts that have deeply influenced my response: (1) I am an African theologian involved in theological education and I currently serve as the Principal of Africa Theological Seminary, and (2) I am a member of the minority Sabaot tribal community, who reside on the slopes of Mt. Elgon, located on the national borders of Kenya and Uganda in Eastern Africa.

I am responding to this paper against the backdrop of the launching of the full Bible into my own native language, the Sabaot, on June 10, 2012. This launch is a culmination of the translation work of Wycliffe Bible Translation (Bible Translation Literacy) that began work on the Sabaot Bible in 1980.

Since the Sabaot people are among the least Christianized people groups in Kenya, I grew up in my rural village accustomed to having the Bible read in Kiswahili (Kenya's national language) and whenever a non-

Sabaot pastor preached, the messages had to undergo translation into my mother tongue. Needless to say, some aspects of the original speaker's messages were often lost in the cross-cultural, linguistic translation.

While the entire Sabaot community is celebrating as they transition from a Bible-less community into one with its own mother tongue Bible, one fact and reality can't escape my attention—the overwhelming statistical evidence that shows even members from communities with the Bible in their own language still do not read the Bible because most people prefer oral learning methods to the literate, printed media approach (Willis and Snowden 2010, 27-28). It is this preceding context that informs my personal passion and inspiration to explore orality as an alternative, effective means of bringing the gospel truth to the hearts of the Sabaot people and the Majority World population that prefer oral learning modes.

A Response to How Should a Theological Institution Prepare Students/Leaders Who Will Go Out into the Field to Train Local People (Storytellers) to Tell Bible Stories Effectively?

Summary of the Paper
Damon So's paper deals with two aspects of orality: (1) describing what it is and (2) exploring ways to improve orality in the context of mission work.

Orality in the Bible and Mission
The author notes that oral forms exist both prior to the writing of scripture and after as the biblical texts were written to be performed orally (i.e., to be read in public gatherings).

In dealing with form and content, the author stresses the importance of ensuring that the content of the biblical message is delivered with cultural sensitivities. Giving an example of Chinese context, So notes that the use of Chinese opera performances in delivering biblical message can prove very effective in contextualizing Christian faith in China.

So also notes the importance of interpreting accurately the original form and meaning of the text to avoid the danger of storytellers propagating heretical teachings. This point confirms the importance of biblically-sound Christian doctrines and interpretations.

Seminary Training

So notes that granted the effectiveness of the oral approach in missions, seminary training should focus on equipping students to train local storytellers in sound biblical interpretation. These local, native storytellers will then propagate the Christian gospel in their own locality using local cultural forms. In preparing the seminary student on orality, he or she should be exposed to the following:

- The oral nature of the biblical narrative itself
- The diverse cultural contexts to which the one form of the Christian gospel should be proclaimed
- The full story of Jesus made possible by the oral approach that overcomes the traditional Western theological approach, which tends to look at one aspect of Jesus' story over the others (e.g., liberals who focus only on the life of Jesus versus conservatives who focus only on the death of Jesus)
- The integration of biblical studies and systematic theology into sound biblical systematic theology that results in a biblical story which is then transmitted into the various cultural audiences in their cultural forms. Thus, the oral approach overcomes the often-overemphasized dichotomy between biblical studies and systematic theology
- In summary, three key interpretations are necessary in transmission of faithful biblical stories: (1) interpretation in biblical studies, (2) integrating biblical studies into systematic theology, and (3) interpreting biblical stories using the oral storytelling in the two points above.

Other Orality Issues

So notes other pertinent issues of orality:

- Skills of performers
- Spirituality of the trainers and the storytellers—nature of Holy Spirit guidance
- Fellowship of trainers and storytellers
- Trainers' willingness to learn and delegate
- Exposing seminary students to field projects on orality
- Exploring cases studies on orality, both negative and positive, for critical study
- Mastering the orality lifecycle: preparations, performance, and evaluations, and then a repeat of the cycle for refined learning process
- The role of explicit interpretation (preaching) after storytelling
- Role of media—radio and TV
- Applying the oral approach in the West so it has the same success it has in non-Western contexts
- Provision of three levels/orders of training: equipping of seminary teachers to train seminary students who in turn train local storytellers

Insights or Discoveries from Paper

Damon So has rightly stressed and highlighted the importance of grounding the oral approach in the sound understanding of the oral nature and form of the biblical narrative itself. Such an emphasis gives sound biblical basis for the theory and practice of orality.

The proposed three-level approach of the seminary's role in equipping for orality—from equipping seminary teachers to training seminary students who in turn train local storytellers—promises to be a productive approach in engaging the seminary as the foundational base in the orality movement. In addition, this seminary-wide approach, which involves faculty and students and is integrated into the existing seminary curriculum, is a better sustainability strategy for orality than the approach of selecting interested members of the seminary community to be involved in orality.

The author correctly points out the importance of integrating sound biblical interpretation in biblical studies with sound systematization of biblical content in systematic theology to get faithful content of the biblical or God story. This is a good deterrent of the heretical teachings that can most easily find its way into the oral approach of the Christian gospel as has happened throughout the Church's history.

This paper clearly shows how the oral approach can help give us the total story of Jesus, which in turn curbs the Western-oriented temptation and bias to focus on one perspective of Jesus' story (either the life of Jesus or the death of Jesus) that has resulted in the emergence of the liberal and conservative wings in the Western Christian tradition.

So's strong emphasis on delivering the oral approach with due consideration of cultural forms or sensitivities is crucial in ensuring the successful delivery of the gospel content to the audiences in their culturally-preferred forms.

Finally, the author highlights other pertinent issues in orality: skills, spirituality, humility, and fellowship of trainers and storytellers; mastering the art of orality such as its lifecycle, exploring case studies, and doing field projects; ways of applying orality in the West; and the role of media (TV and radio) in the oral approach.

Missing Gaps and Challenges

The paper is quite good in discussing the overall strategy of providing a theoretical framework for the seminary's role in orality, but it does not identify specifics and details of how the same can be achieved in the seminary setting. Thus, there is no indication of how the curriculum or syllabus can be reviewed in relation to the proposals presented.

After suggesting the role of orality in integrating two key seminary departments, the author falls short of clarifying and detailing how the seminary's departmental divisions of biblical studies and systematic theology departments can be eradicated or broken down through the introduction of the oral approach of learning gospel content.

As already hinted in the paper, So does not deal with the specifics or details of identifying the resources seminary students use in the training of storytellers; qualities of trainers and storytellers; the nature of field projects in orality training; and practical ways or avenues of applying orality in Western contexts.

Finally, the paper does not mention the importance of the seminary engaging in partnerships and networking with stakeholders involved in orality (pastors already on the field and parachurch organizations dealing with orality) who will strategically provide logistical, moral, and resource-based support to the seminary's training on orality.

Questions Emerging from the Paper

1. In what practical way can seminaries adjust or integrate their departments of biblical studies and systematic theology through introducing an oral approach?

2. What criteria will seminary students trained in orality use to identify the local storytellers to be trained and sent to tell the biblical story? What resources shall they use in training the storytellers?

3. To what extent should seminary faculty be involved in field projects on orality? How effective will the faculty training be if they don't participate in the training or evaluation of the storytellers?

4. How should the seminaries work with pastors who are not seminary students and churches at the grassroots level, where most storytelling is practiced through preaching and teaching ministry?

5. What plans should seminaries have in place to meet the needs of pastors on the field who need training and resources to apply the oral approach in their ministries?

A Response to Africa Theological Seminary
Summary of the Paper

Phil Walker gives a good introductory background and overview of Africa Theological Seminary (ATS).

Orality and Theological Education

Walker notes that orality is not just a strategy to reach the oral learners, but rather an ongoing issue of evaluating how learners process information and learn. He gives three key issues that orality raises when it comes to how we should do theological education:

- Giving primary oral learners strategy to plant churches and disciple without using print media
- Targeting secondary oral learners (i.e., the majority of ATS staff, faculty, and students) with skills and resources for reaching out to the non-literate oral learners
- Understanding that orality has roots in the unconscious brain which recent scientific research has identified as the root of all human behavior. The traditional approach to learning has little impact on the unconscious part of the brain. However, stories reach to this unconscious brain as it provides schemas or framework upon which behavior is directed, so story impacts the unconscious brain, which in turn influences behavior. Values and virtues must be expressed behaviorally and this can be done with the aid of four actions: Focus, Feedback, Intensity, and Time.

ATS's Approach to Integrating Orality

Walker lists three key areas in which ATS seeks to integrate orality:

- Relationship to primary oral learners. Here, strategy is two-fold: (a) to work with ION East Africa towards developing training programs to target Christian leaders working among Bible-less communities, especially the Sabaot community. This training is aimed to take place at the certificate level; and (b) incorporating oral learning styles in all study programs.
- Relationship to secondary oral learners. ATS seeks to link up with its students, faculty, and staff by adjusting their teaching approach to include orality; introducing a core course on orality and integrating orality into teaching of other courses; entering into partnerships with orality organizations to avail resources for oral learners and practitioners; incorporating orality into the graded student field projects—20 percent of each course; six to eight hours of field practicum in all ATS formal programs; and building an institutional culture in which oral means are used to pass on core beliefs, values, and virtues.
- Impact on character and transformation of learners. The ATS approach is used to see how the use of oral means of story, drama, and song reinforces God's story, which in turn helps the unconscious mind to form a grid for behavior or character formation. ATS does this through its various extra-curricular discipleship programs in order to help build an institutional culture of transformation. These include building devotions around Bible stories; living Christian values in the day-to-day seminary life; accountability groups; and focusing on one or two core values or virtues in a given term/semester to reinforce character formation priority.

Insights from ATS' Approach of Integrating Orality into Theological Education

- ATS' approach for a system-wide participation that includes staff and faculty in orientation is vital since leadership must model any new approach for it to succeed. Staff and faculty are crucial in ensuring the adoption of this new approach to teaching and preaching the gospel. Without them, such new approaches may not get the needed support for sustainability.

- ATS' planned overhaul of the way faculty teach to include incorporating orality approaches is vital. This is because faculty members teach best by modeling and students are best instructed by observing what and how their teacher performs and conducts him or herself.

- The ATS approach to use orality in its teaching approach called "Synergogy"—blended model between andragogy and pedagogy—is an insight worth considering in ensuring the teacher-student interaction that is key to orality is well integrated into the teaching process.

- The ATS approach to establish one core course on theory and methods of orality and then reinforce orality into a teaching approach in other courses sounds like a good strategy to help learners to be acquainted and be equipped with knowledge and skills of integrating orality into their ministries.

  The establishment of an orality resource center at ATS through partnership with key providers of resources on orality (such as Davar, etc.) is a great way to link its students, alumni, faculty, staff, library users, and other interested ATS stakeholders with contacts and the latest information on all issues related to orality. In addition, such an orality resource hub will show interested parties the orality resources available. This approach will fill in the oft-missing gap of potential partners not knowing what to get or where and how to get the orality resources.

- Finally, ATS' approach to use orality as a means to build the institutional culture of character transformation by integrating it into its discipleship programs is insightful since orality impacts the unconscious brain, which dictates human behavior. This insight is worth considering and pursuing as an important component in reinforcing the effectiveness of orality in achieving character transformation.

Missing Gaps and Challenges

- As the author has alluded, there is an urgent need to explore ways in which the entire ATS curriculum can be overhauled to ensure that the lecturers' approach incorporates orality skills and that student participation and assessment criteria give room to issues pertinent to orality. It is important to rethink the entire ATS syllabus in light of integrating orality. A good starting point would be to begin integrating orality into the syllabus of practical or general ministry division courses such as Homiletics, Expository Preaching, Christian Education, Marriage & Family, etc.

- There is a need for ATS to consider appointing a coordinator at the faculty level to see that the institutional approach to orality is published widely and implemented as per the guidelines provided by key organs of the institution. Such a move demonstrates the seriousness the institution attaches to the orality approach to presenting the gospel.

- There is need for ATS to consider how they can integrate orality with its Alumni Association ministry. As an interdenominational institution, ATS alumni constitute an important link to the church network at the grassroots level that will assist in ensuring adoption of this approach in the churches. Furthermore, since all ATS students are practitioners in ministry, it would be strategic for ATS to use current students to introduce orality into the students' ongoing ministries as they learn its skills in the seminary.

- There is a need for ATS to link up with ION East Africa in implementing the Church-based Oral Bible Schools (OBS). This can be done using its student body and two existing departments. A few points here. First, as an in-service institution, all ATS students study as they continue ministry. It is quite strategic to use students to set up OBS in their churches and ministries. Second, the Alumni Association currently has over 1,000 alumni members who can use their church ministry locations as OBS centers. Third, ATS has a Christian Leadership Institute (CLI), which offers short-term church-based seminars and workshops. The CLI's existing network can form a vital starting point for incorporating orality by sensitizing church leaders and churches to the importance of orality, as well as train and equip interested leaders on the effectiveness of orality in the church's overall discipleship, outreach, and evangelism programs.

- ATS' proposed approach to adopt orality only at the certificate level may be a good initial approach, but it may not have the desired broad impact in the end. As Walker has pointed out, the system-wide approach is more effective, and this I believe means integrating orality into the formal programs at all levels that ATS programs are offered.

Questions for Consideration

1. What plans does ATS have in involving church leaders beyond its institution as a strategy for influencing the leaders at the grassroots level to integrate orality into their ministries?

2. How is ATS planning to use its existing alumni and CLI network to promote orality as an effective approach in discipleship and church-planting ministries?

3. Granted that ATS is an in-service institution which allows students to study as they continue their ministries, is ATS considering implementing church-based Oral Bible Schools using this network of student pastors?

A Response to Oral Bible Story Telling Training at New India
Bible Seminary, Kerala, India
Mary Verghese states:

- There is an important link between orality and its ability to overcome contexts that prohibit public evangelistic programs and activities.
- There is a vital link between orality and its effectiveness in reaching Bible-less communities.
- There is a key weakness of translations from one language to another as transferring the mindset of the preacher which further confuses the recipient.

Partnerships in the Orality Movement

The partnerships between New India Evangelistic Association (NIEA), New India Bible School (NIBS), Last Commandment Initiative (LCI), and other orality-based or-supporting organizations have provided a widespread networking that has resulted in increased church planting and Christianization.

Availing Resources

NIEA's development of Bible storying resources is vital in making the gospel available to unreached communities.

Role of NIBS in Orality

Training NIBS students to acquaint with OBS techniques and as a tool for mission strategy

Future Vision: Have an orality department at NIBS; make orality a module course at BTh; and do bi-annual OBS training in July and October; train NIBS graduates as OBS facilitators in their respective fields in partnership with LCI.

Challenges of NIBS Partnerships in Orality

NIBS' program promises greater chances for sustainability of the program through partnership with key organizations, especially LCI, and through its commitment to dedicated NIBS graduates for the long-term ministry to oral learners. The appointment of a NIBS coordinator for this program, submission to LCI supervision of the graduates signed up and paying a stipend to enrolled graduates increases the chances for sustainability of the program for the long term.

A well-planned curriculum for orientation and training of NIBS graduates as OBS interns guarantees sharpened skills in orality. The on-the-job training is also helpful in providing continued support for the interns.

Missing Gaps and Challenges

As hinted by Verghese, there is a need to develop a concrete plan to integrate orality into the formal or core courses in NIBS' formal study programs. This will require a comprehensive review of the NIBS' curriculum.

Verghese suggests plans to integrate orality into the accredited BTh program alone. Further, NIBS' approach is keen to select the right, interested team of students and train them further in orality in order to serve as OBS facilitators. In my humble opinion, if NIBS' desire is to include effectively the… the entire student population in orientation to orality, it seems most strategic to consider including orality as one core course, or at least a component in the graded part of all the formal programs offered by NIBS. This point is informed by the fact that students often take more seriously a graded program than one offered as an enrichment program without earned grades.

There is one key missing gap in NIBS' orality program—that of non-involvement of NIBS faculty in the OBS orientation training program. As opinion shapers, faculty are crucial in ensuring the needed support for the program by encouraging the students to be involved, as well as integrating skills for including oral learners in mission strategy for the entire theological training process in the seminary. As a suggestion, faculty can be included at the orientation phase and as mentoring or supervising agents for students or graduates enrolled as OBST facilitators.

NIBS' approach to orality seems heavily dependent upon networking with NIEA and para-church organizations and little with the local, indigenous church networks. Granted that churches' mission and mandate is to reach oral learners with the gospel, wouldn't it make strategic sense to include them in the networking strategy?

NIBS' program does not indicate the sources of curriculum resourcing—is it NIBS faculty? Or is it the role of the partnering organizations? If the latter, then great care should be taken to ensure the program does not fail due to misinterpretation of the partnership agreements, and that the partner organization does not fail to meet its obligations in the partnership agreement.

Questions for Consideration at Consultation and Future of NIBS' Approach to Orality

1. How is NIBS going to produce training resources for OBST?
2. Are there plans for NIBS faculty to be involved in the program? If so, to what extent is the faculty involvement for the success and sustainability of OBST program?
3. Is NIBS considering an approach to orality beyond networking with parachurch organizations?
4. What is NIBS' strategy to work with churches at the grassroots level, where most preaching and teaching ministry interfaces with the ordinary Christian populace?
5. What plans does NIBS have to meet the needs of pastors who simply need resources and skills to implement the orality strategies in their ministries?

Conclusion

As an African whose basic and natural learning mode and orientation is oral, matters of oral learning strike to the heart of my being. I find great comfort in the fact that the modern orality movement is challenging us to retrieve this natural learning orientation that we often see in children's learning processes, but from which Western learning styles and approaches diverged. It will require a long-term re-orientation to move toward oral approaches to learning, as well as concerted effort of key stakeholders to reverse such an orientation to learning.

It is for this reason that I fully agree with Walker's take on how theological educators and theological institutions can form the hope of making this worthwhile transformation by offering the credibility and validity to move orality to the center of theological discourse. I thus conclude by quoting Walker:

> If theological institutions cannot or will not provide the credibility and the validity of the model, then it will remain a phenomenon used by missionaries and others working in societies made up of primary oral learners. We, in the formal theological educational arena, have the power and the ability to provide the credibility that will move the movement from periphery to the center of discipleship. But we must act now to draw the model into the essence of our training.
> *(from Chapter 2, Africa Theological Seminary, p. 47—48)*

PERSPECTIVE II:

Non-Formal Education—
Training Organizations and the
Oral Preference Learner

We have undoubtedly been challenged from the previous Perspective: *What is the role of contextualization with scripture and the world of cultures? How do we handle the dialectical tensions? Is the role of the teacher changing to become facilitator or validator? Where is our starting point, and what is the role of accreditation? How can we possibly have faculty and staff integration?*

As if those are not sufficient, now we move into Perspective II. During the consultation, participants dialogued about the "whole Bible."

What is the meta-narrative, and how does the whole move to the part, and where does this training lead?

Or, if the parts make the whole, but what is the whole that the parts describe?

Furthermore, in conducting training on the "whole counsel" of the Word of God, is the reference to the content from God's word more of a content quantity or something more qualitative?

Finally, what is the trainers' role in determining if someone has learned? What is the process for evaluating growth?

Again, we ask you to consider your experiences. As you read through this section with a small group of colleagues and friends, consider how you can add this Perspective to the one you have just read.

Chapter 5

Multiplying Disciples in an Oral Context

Jackson Atkins

Jesus once told his followers, "The harvest is plentiful, but the laborers are few. Therefore pray earnestly to the Lord of the harvest to send out laborers into his harvest" (Matt. 10:2). Jesus' words ring as true today as they did when he spoke them the first time. The world currently has seven billion inhabitants, but far too few laborers to work these fields.

The last 150 years have seen a revolution in missionary activity, yet the Church has been hard-pressed to keep up with the exploding population. People now realize the great need for each Christian disciple to reproduce him or herself. Only through this multiplication of workers will the Church make great headway in reaching the vast throngs of those who live without Christ. Many champion the idea of multiplication, yet it seems sometimes quite elusive. In this paper, we will explore some of the factors behind the multiplication of disciples and offer insights from the field on multiplying disciples in oral contexts.

Why Multiplication Happens

Multiplication happens based upon two factors: *motivation and ease of transfer*. In other words, people replicate because they want to pass on what they have, and they are able to pass it on. Formal theological education is highly valuable. The professors and teachers are highly motivated to pass on what they have. However, a MDiv degree usually takes three years of full-time study to complete, which many people are not able to do. Seminary teachers are replicating themselves, but they do so very slowly because the complex subject matter is difficult to transfer.

The opposite is also true. The simplest gospel presentation is to say, "Jesus is Lord." Anyone could be trained to do this and tell others to do this in less than one minute. This simple proclamation is very easy to transfer. Yet people do not teach this as an evangelism method because they are not motivated to use this method. Why? Because this simple method gets few results. No one wants to pass on something he or she does not think works. If we want to see replication in the field, we must use methods that people want to use and can pass on easily.

People are motivated by two primary factors: *their personal spiritual health and how they perceive the effectiveness of what they are doing*. People with hard hearts might be presented with an extremely effective method of evangelism; yet, they might not use it because they are not concerned about lost people's salvation. On the other hand, people with great spiritual maturity who yearn to see people know Christ might quit using an evangelistic method because they do not think it works.

Digging Deep into Scripture

We have found that teaching people how to "dig deep" into scripture to find and present spiritual treasures is a key to motivating others to multiply. Digging deep means people find and apply the spiritual truths beyond those found on the surface. It is not unusual for oral learners to find up to 15 spiritual truths in a five to ten-verse story.

Digging deep motivates people to replicate because it affects both factors in motivation. It grows people spiritually and people perceive that it is highly effective. As people dig deep into scripture, they are challenged or encouraged by the Holy Spirit in new ways. The Spirit uses scripture to draw people closer to God. As people mature spiritually, they grow in love for their fellow people and they appreciate God's desire to reach and disciple all people. This personal spiritual growth creates a desire within people to replicate.

People also perceive that digging deep into scripture is highly effective. On the field, we often see this perception start within the individual. We hear comments like, "God spoke to me in this story" or "There is far more in the Bible than I ever thought." One pastor from South America commented, "People in my country say they don't want to hear stories; they want theology. I went to Bible school and seminary to learn to preach this way. Now I see there is so much theology in the stories." His eyes were opened!

When people dig deep, they are changed and they want to go and teach others. When they see the results in others, they are even more motivated. Recently, one pastor in the United States said his church changed from a traditional Sunday night service to small groups using an oral method that focuses on digging deep. He commented, "Our attendance has doubled! The people are hungrier for the word than they have ever been." He now wants to be a part of a team training other churches to do the same. The truths of scripture touched him and those to whom he ministers. Now he is motivated to replicate himself.

Finding the Treasures in Scripture

Finding these treasures in God's word motivates people to replicate. But how do people discover these treasures? People find spiritual truths by listening closely to the story. They must listen to the story closely when they prepare the story and then help their hearers listen well to the story by asking targeted questions.

People prepare to tell the story using an inductive approach that leads to finding the spiritual treasures. This process **begins with the storyteller asking two questions about the whole story**. First, the storyteller asks if anything happened before this Bible story that might make it more understandable. This question places a Bible story within its proper context. The story where the Israelites grumble and complain that "there is no food and no water" would make little sense without knowing that God gave them manna from heaven six days a week and had provided them water for nearly 40 years (Num. 21:4-9).

Next, the storyteller asks about the situation or circumstance of the whole story. This question aims to help the storyteller not miss the main point of the story and to create an emotional connection with the characters. The person preparing wants to understand what it might be like to be someone in the story.

After the storyteller has asked these two questions of the whole story, he or she continues preparing by **going through the story slowly, section by section, asking the same series of questions in each part**. The storyteller asks, "In this section, what can I learn spiritually about the characters from what they are saying or doing? Did any of the characters make a choice and if they did what other choices could they have made? In this section, do I see any results from their choices, and was anyone impacted? Finally, where and how is God working in this circumstance?"

Breaking the story into sections and asking these questions forces the storyteller to move slowly through the story and look at each character and his or her decisions. Without this discipline, people often skip to the highlights of the story and miss some of the wonderful treasures which lie deeper in the story.

Now that the storyteller has prepared a Bible story by listening well, he or she is ready to present the story. The storyteller **goes through the story three times in different ways to fix the story into the listeners' minds**. Then, the storyteller **asks gentle questions** that help the hearers listen well to the story and find spiritual treasures for themselves.

The storyteller picks out some of the treasures he or she finds and goes back to his or her preparation time to remember what part of the story his or her treasure came from and what questions helped the storyteller find the treasure. The storyteller then repeats that part of the story and asks the same questions that helped him or her find the treasure. This allows the listeners to experience the same joy of discovering the truth that the storyteller experienced.

After helping the hearers discover the truths, the storyteller helps them apply the truths through a series of application questions. These questions include: "Today, does this still happen? In what ways does this still happen? Has this ever happened to you or someone you know? Will you share your experience? What in this story might help you if this happened to you in the future?"

This slow search for spiritual treasures yields many wonderful insights into scripture which might otherwise be passed over. This intentional process of going slow to find the treasures and apply them changes individuals and communities. This transformational change motivates people to multiply themselves.

Transferring Information and Skills

However, multiplication is made up of more than motivation. For people to replicate themselves quickly, they must be able to transfer information and skills easily. The ease of this transfer is made up of two factors—the simplicity of the material and the method used to teach the material. The inductive approach outlined earlier is more complicated than some of techniques for studying the scriptures because it involves dividing the story into parts. Yet this method is far simpler than many methods currently used.

The way the technique is taught makes a huge impact on how easily it is transferred. If we taught the process of digging deep by using highly literate approaches like an outline, we would see little reproduction among oral learners. We have found it to be very effective to use oral techniques to train oral learners how to prepare and present their stories. Thus, the training itself is oral.

We wrap our key teachings in stories, we model the methods, and we provide opportunities for learners to put their skills into practice during the training and receive personalized coaching. Thus, the whole training is oral and more easily transferred.

For example, we teach the process for inductive study outlined above by telling a story about some villagers who have a dispute about a well. These villagers go to a wise counselor and ask advice. After hearing their story, the wise counselor asks, "Tell me in just a few words what is your problem?" Then he asks, "Did anything happen before this dispute that might help me understand it?" After the villagers answer these questions, the wise counselor says, "Tell me your story again but this time tell it slowly." After the villagers tell the first part of their story, the wise counselor says, "Stop. Now in just this part did any of you say anything or do anything that might help me understand? In this part, did any of you make choices and could you have made any different choices? If you made a choice, what was the result and who was impacted?"

After the villagers answer the questions, the wise counselor asks them to continue to tell their story. When the villagers tell the next part, the wise counselor again stops them and asks the same set of questions. After the villagers and the wise counselor go through the whole story of their dispute part by part, the wise counselor is able to give good advice because he has asked many questions and listened.

This is an oral presentation of the same information that was given earlier in a literate form. We have seen fifth-generation learners who are able to accurately retell this story and apply this technique to a passage of scripture.

Modeling

Modeling has also proven to be a critical technique for passing on skills. One major component of the training process we use is teaching people how to train the next generation. We tried passing on this skill through lecture. We told these trainees all the things they should be doing, but many left confused and not ready to bring along the next generation.

Now we have implemented a skit where the trainees watch a master instructor lead a group of newcomers. The trainees see an excellent model of what they should be doing. This model answers many of their questions and we have seen a significant improvement in their ability to teach the next generation. We have also experimented by having a master instructor stand before the group and prepare a story out loud as they would on their own. The instructor says what he or she might normally only be thinking. This exercise has greatly helped learners understand how to prepare a story when they are on their own.

Doing

Finally, people learn best by doing. During the training session each person has the opportunity to prepare, tell the story and lead discussion with a live group, and receive personalized coaching. In the same way, those who come to learn how to train others are given the chance to lead a group through the process of preparation. Many attendees have commented that they "got it" when they began to teach others.

Using oral methods within the training presents some difficulties. It is more time consuming and difficult to write a story about what to do then it is to give people a list of steps. The story of the wise counselor took several years and many iterations to develop. Oral methods often take longer on the front end. It takes less time to tell people what they should do when they teach others how to prepare a story than it does to have a master instructor do a demonstration.

However, these difficulties are worth fighting through. Using the story to teach the process has greatly increased how fast people understand and pass on the information. Although the demonstrations take more time up front, this time is easily recuperated because people understand better what to do and they have fewer questions.

The fields are white for a harvest of souls into God's kingdom. We have a responsibility to raise up more workers to go into these fields. Multiplying ourselves and teaching others how to multiply will play a critical role in creating enough workers. We can motivate people into the harvest fields by giving them tools which lead to spiritual transformation in their own lives and the lives of those they reach. We can then equip them to multiply by using simple techniques that are taught in oral ways such as stories, demonstrations, hands-on practice, and personal coaching. In this way, the Church will make great inroads into reaching the vast numbers of unreached people from our backyards to the ends of the earth.

Chapter 6

Orality Applied in a Classroom Setting with Amazon Region Indian Students

David Irving

In the fall of 1990, still newlyweds, my wife, Fran, and I were called to work full time with the Jarawara tribe in one of their villages. After learning the basics of the Jarawara language, we began to translate and share stories from the Bible.

Over the next 15 years, isolated from other missionaries and ignorant of much of what was happening in missionary education, we continued using both oral and more traditional teaching methods among the Jarawara. Starting about 1986, other YWAM mission teams tried some of the same methods, also isolated and working, like us, pretty much on their own. We rarely met together during those years. This happened not because of jealousy, but more because of a lack of overall leadership and initiative.

This changed in 2005, when several mission teams began to meet together to pray, dream, and plan for a school which would begin the next year and be open to indigenous students from all Brazilian tribes. We settled on the name EMPA, which means Multi-ethnic School for Adults.

Values in the Brazilian Culture

Our vision in 2005 was of a classroom setting different from any with which we were familiar, where the teaching methods and values used would reflect teaching methods and values basic to the indigenous cultures of Brazil. One such value is **informality**. Whether the moment is of a wedding, burial, birth, coming of age party, or church service, there is almost never a ceremony. Adults and children alike arrive at the event with a very casual, relaxed attitude. Many arrive after the appointed time. Usually, children and adults continue conversing until the main speaker starts speaking and sometimes afterwards. Children and babies are welcome and present everywhere. They are never excluded from any event, situation, or meeting. Their parents take them out only when they continue crying.

In traditional North Amazon region tribal cultures, strong, win-at-whatever-cost competitiveness is not an important value. Several eyewitness experiences have vividly demonstrated this on more than one occasion.

Years ago, Fran and I wanted to put on an athletic competition for the enjoyment of the Jarawara community. As part of this competition, we included a footrace among the middle-aged men. At the sound of the whistle, they started off, each running his maximum. A minute or so later, as they approached the finish line, we witnessed what for us was a very strange sight. In spite of the fact that he was out in front, Waka visibly slowed down, thus allowing at least two other men to catch up and cross the finish line with him. A very similar experience happened in the neighboring Banawa village.

Another important oral culture value is **repetitiveness**. Whether it is an everyday conversation or the old chief telling a story that occurred in his grandfather's time, the speaker repeats the main idea or main verb of the clause, often many times.

Another factor to be considered in a classroom setting is the common practice of **finishing another person's sentence or conversation**. Where there is more than one participant to an event, another person may very well interrupt the first speaker anywhere in his or her discourse. When this happens, it is not considered bad manners, but rather is seen as normal behavior, thus allowing the participation of a larger number of speakers.

While we planned to use orality in a classroom setting, orality was one of several means in preparing indigenous students to become productive citizens of Brazil.

After our first successful year in 2006, some of our EMPA staff took the basic One Story training course and began implementing important One Story principles into our schools. One Story, an initiative in orality managed by CRU, International Mission Board, Trans World Radio, Wycliffe International, and Youth With A Mission, helped us to become more organized and focused.

Basic Outline of the Classroom Session

A typical classroom session starts after **an hour of prayer and praise**, during which the teachers and students sing several songs, some in Portuguese and others in the various represented tribal languages. The students have composed many of the praise songs without any formal music training whatsoever. Along with the praise songs, several teachers, primarily during the first two years, have composed music about the different Brazilian school subjects: Bible, geography, history, Portuguese, anatomy, and others. The classrooms, although simple in construction, are open, well ventilated, and cheery, and decorated with drawings, charts, and maps.

As the class starts, the children are present on their parents' laps or close by. The children enjoy the praise time, even actively singing along. They are also welcome for the first hour of class time, when the teachers tell the first stories. Present too, in many instances, are the missionaries who work with each tribal group. These missionaries help to explain words or phrases unfamiliar to the students and translate whenever necessary.

The person directing the first story gives a brief introduction and then begins telling the story. The stories are always relatively short, no more than five to seven minutes in length. Before telling the story, the storyteller needs to memorize it, being sure to share the important values within the story and avoiding the inclusion of any personal opinions or other additions.

It is important, whenever possible, to choose the best possible storyteller. Someone who is expressive generally does a better job of maintaining the interest of the audience. A good storyteller may use gestures, body movements, facial expressions, different voices; but at the same time must speak slowly and enunciate clearly. He or she must also look at the audience.

After the storyteller tells the story once, he or she may tell it again, neither adding nor subtracting anything. Generally after this, one of the students will retell the same story in his or her own words, followed by another student.

We never felt it was essential that the student retelling the story should have to retell all of it, remembering to perfection all of the details. If two or three students helped each other, together retelling the story, this too was valid. By listening to the students, we have a good idea whether or not the students have been able to follow the story.

The next step might be to **show a related video clip, or to present the same story as a dramatization**, using as actors a combination of students and teachers, or even other people not necessarily involved in the school.

Several times during this entire process, **the teacher directing the class asks if everyone understands the story**. By this time, the children leave with their teachers to begin activities designed for their age group.

By now it might be time for a **pause of 15-20 minutes** to use the bathroom and have a snack—typical indigenous foods such as macaxeira or sweet potato. After the break, the students return to the classroom.

During the second morning session, writing is the focus. The teachers divide the students into **smaller groups** according to level. Each small group is accompanied by a teacher. First, the teacher reads a short text based upon the story one or two times, each time remembering to enunciate clearly and not to read too fast. Then, several students, one by one, read the story or text, either from the blackboard or from an individual copy. After this, the students copy the text into their notebooks.

In the afternoon sessions, the students participate in games or competitions based upon the day's story. The students might also have computer or guitar classes. At night, there are no classes.

The teachers try to include as many physically participative activities as possible. For example, during a history class about useful inventions from ancient civilizations, we set off a big skyrocket after hearing about gunpowder. (Unfortunately, our neighbors from another mission, who had no idea what was happening, mistakenly thought an electrical transformer had exploded.)

Studying about cuneiform writing, we gave each student an amount of clay that he or she patted into a thin layer. Then, the student cut one end of a stick into a triangle shape and wrote his or her name like the Sumerians. After the class, each student placed his or her clay tablet to dry in the sun.

Challenges and Encouragement

We have witnessed many more positive than negative manifestations of tribal cultural values in the classroom setting. Typically, any time a teacher calls on a student to answer a question or a student volunteers, if he or she answers correctly, the other students clap their hands in appreciation and encouragement. Even if the student answers incorrectly or fails to answer at all, the other students will applaud. If he or she becomes stuck or confused, the other students will tell him or her the right answer, thus helping the student avoid embarrassment.

A major problem we have found with orality as a teaching tool is that for the student who is already familiar with hearing the story repeated in a necessarily simplified form, class time can be a mind-numbing, unstimulating experience. In addition, for the teaching team responsible for preparing the classes, having to come up with varied and creative ways of communicating subject matter day after day, the task may become tiring and ultimately overwhelming.

In spite of the problems, orality as a teaching method has been an overwhelming success in transforming lives. The national Brazilian government now employs several of the best students from the early years of EMPA as teachers and health workers. In the past seven years, many students at the different multicultural schools have decided to follow Christ, and, at the end of each year, have been baptized in the Madeira river near the Porto Velho YWAM base.

However, what better testimony than to hear Dioneia Freitas, current EMPA Director, and several students, share what EMPA and EMBI (Multi-Ethnic Bible School) mean to them:

"For the people of oral tradition, orality is the best method to reach them. But it needs to be contextualized orality using simple language." (Dioneia Freitas)

"EMPA helped me to speak better Portuguese and to respect others. EMBI helped me to understand more about God. These two schools transformed my life." (Neme Jarawara)

"They taught us the good news about God. The schools helped my math and Portuguese. They opened our minds. They taught us in a way so we can pass it on to others in other villages." (Bonita Jarawara)

"Before EMPA I didn't know Portuguese. They taught me Portuguese and math. In EMBI they taught the word of God. And they taught us to respect others and our parents." (Mamani Jarawara)

"During EMBI I learned more about the things of God, good things." (Aiti Jarawara)

Without a doubt, orality will continue to be an essential teaching tool worldwide.

Chapter 7

A Response to the Articles in Perspective II

Miriam Adeney

What Is Enough?
Oral Bible Teaching in Three Dimensions

Mark Rich was my mother's cousin thrice removed. When he was 23 years old, and already the father of two little girls, he was captured by FARC guerillas of Colombia. A few days later, the New Tribes Mission received a ransom request for $5 million for him and two others. We prayed for Mark for years. But, in the end, Mark, Dave, and Rich were killed.

One FARC member who was with them in the guerilla camp was a man named Alberto. He himself had suffered profoundly. When he was 11, the local militia raped his mother and sisters and murdered all of his family. No one extended a hand to him except the guerillas. To be with them, he had to kill. For the next quarter century, that was his life.

Yet today, Alberto is a brother in Christ. Why? Because Mark, Dave, and Rich bathed him with scripture from morning to night. Their Bibles were burned, yet they kept quoting verses. They kept singing, even when they shook from malaria. "Great

Is Thy Faithfulness" rang out through the jungle right up to the end.

During Alberto's months with them, the word of God was carved into his brain. Today, his testimony is one long stream of scripture, alternating with songs that he internalized. Biblical ignorance may be widespread in the U.S., but apparently it was no problem for this FARC killer. Oral teaching made the difference. That is why we are participating in this conference: to serve the millions of people like Alberto.

I have been asked to respond to two papers. David Irving's paper describes Amazon jungle Bible schools where the teaching media include stories, tribal language and Portuguese songs, extended prayer, dramas, videos, action learning through projects and experiments, and literacy and writing classes. Students express thanks for learning more about God, as well as Portuguese and math.

In Jackson Atkins' paper, he focuses on telling a story framed by guiding questions. *What would it be like to be a person in the story? he asks. Did anything happen earlier that would help us understand this better? What choices do these persons make? What if they made other choices? Where is God working here? Do things like this happen today? What are the treasures in this story?* First, Atkins considers the story as a whole, then applies the questions section by section. He teaches by modeling, and now has teachers using this method extending into the fifth generation.

Both papers provide excellent suggestions, Irving at the macro level and Atkins at the micro level. I will add a few comments, organized in three sections. (For my most specific comments, go directly to section three.)

Good Methods Are Not Enough: What We Teach about God

Orality is not new in Christian communication. Moses and Jesus and many missionaries throughout history used it. Yet today, while oral creations are appreciated for holidays or for pre-evangelism, core teaching in church and mission often remains didactic, linear, and print-based.

There is some justification for this. Bible teachers know that without balanced understanding of God, heresies may develop. Nor can we love God or our neighbor well over time without a broad kingdom worldview.

Do storytellers provide that? Storytellers are artists—usually they don't think systematically. That is not their call. They are absorbed with the trees, not the forest. Aware of this, Bible teachers may sideline stories as "theology lite."

To be credible in mission circles, then, the orality initiative must prove that we unite system with story. In Irving's and Atkins' papers, I had hoped to see this stated. The challenge is to transmit the WHOLE counsel of God using appropriate media. The ball is in our court. We must show that comprehensive balanced teaching can occur through imaginative genres.

There is documentary evidence. Take the case of 17 North Africans who were taught a sequence of 135 Bible stories. After two years, a seminary professor gave them a six-hour exam. Could they connect the stories with core doctrines, with basic themes of the faith? Indeed, they could. Given a theological theme, they quickly referred to multiple stories. They answered doctrinal questions with illustrations.

In both Atkins' and Irving's communities, it is quite possible that such comprehensive, balanced teaching occurs. If so, that needs to be stated. We cannot take it for granted. Worldwide—not least in the American Church—there is so much biblical ignorance, so much superficial and skewed understanding. John Stott once said, "All our preaching, week in and week out, should gradually unfold the 'whole counsel of God' and so contribute to the development of Christian minds in the congregation."

We have a similar call. From Genesis to Revelation, from the Father to Jesus to the Holy Spirit to human nature to the Church to last things, what do our people know? What are we teaching? As an anthropologist, I love indigenous oral art genres. But I love scripture more. Method does not trump message. In every orality paper, then, we need to state that the balanced teaching of the whole counsel of God is our goal, not just snippets of scripture, however interesting they may be. Such continual reiteration would reassure the conventional Bible teachers and would keep the artists and the neophyte teachers—and ourselves—centered on our big Story with all its diverse parts gathered together in Christ.

Good Theology Is Not Enough: What We Learn about Culture

Beyond theology, knowing a culture's patterns should influence the story themes we accent. This means more than connecting to surface traits. It means systematic analysis of the culture. Routinely, when we prepare to teach, we should review economic patterns, social network patterns, value patterns, and histories of oppression. Yet I see no mention of this in these two papers.

For example, in the **social sphere**, there are patterns for births, marriages, funerals, and maybe coming-of-age events. There are customary ways to handle conflicts between individuals, families, or groups, as well as generational tensions. Surely, these should affect what stories we select and how we develop them.

In the **economic sphere**, there are borrowing and lending arrangements, some obligatory and some optional. Some people's work will show profit and growth. Others will struggle, and maybe fall into debt, and maybe fail. Some will be exploited or cheated by international or national powers. Some will leave to find work elsewhere. Family members who remain behind will be lonely and will have to restructure their lives. In such situations, women who become de facto heads of households may experience new empowerment. These realities, too, should shape our stories.

In the **recreational sphere**, there are patterned celebrations, artistic creativity, sports, and perhaps outdoor activities that are partly economic and partly recreational. In the arena of modernity, media broadens knowledge and connections, but also introduces materialistic desires, foreign lifestyles, and pornography, weakening the community. Like other parts of culture, the patterned effects of such transnational influences can be documented.

In the **church**, believers may want to learn more about evangelism, discipling, teaching, administration, counseling, finances, children's ministry, youth work, leader training, discipline, curriculum development, charity, sustainable development, or advocacy.

How do we select "teaching stories?" We choose them and plan their development after systematic analysis of the cultural context. Irving does mention cultural elements that affect his teaching, such as noncompetitiveness, finishing others' sentences, or repeating the main idea or verb many times. Beyond these selected specifics, I'd like to hear how the stories chosen systematically speak to the culture's core patterns. At least I'd like to hear that this is a habitual practice.

Storytelling is a teachable craft, but it is more than technique. It is communication to persons whose thoughts and feeling are shaped by certain patterns. Different cultures bring different questions to scripture. "Local theologies" develop these. Take, for example, the titles of the 60 short articles listed in the *Africa Bible Commentary's* Table of Contents. Would any American commentary contain essays on "Female Genital Mutilation," "Initiation Rites," "The Role of Ancestors," "Widow Inheritance," or "Tribalism, Ethnicity, and Race?"

Contexts differ. Therefore, story selections and emphases must differ, based upon wise study of the culture.

Good Content Is Not Enough: Methods Matter

Of course, appropriate media matter. Here I have three comments.

Connotations and denotations in oral art. To get at the meat of a Bible story, Atkins poses a set of analytical questions. Some are noted in the beginning of this paper. This approach has proved effective. Nevertheless, does this emphasis on denotative meaning do justice to connotative communication?

There are nonverbal aspects to oral art. Some concern art style. Others concern social performance etiquette. Who tells stories in this society? Where and when? Do people of different ages or social classes or genders discuss matters freely together? Or do they need separate groups?

More fundamentally, is analysis admired, or is the preservation of mystery preferred? Could explicit analysis ever "kill" a story? "Only an uncouth person needs a direct, verbal, complete message," says anthropologist Takie Sugiyama Lebra, speaking of Japanese, but representing indirect communicators everywhere. "A person of aesthetic refinement and sophistication sends indirect, implicit, subtle messages." Words to the wise. Is there a time to analyze, and a time to let the story shimmer without shredding?

Regarding art style, many cultures have sophisticated multidimensional criteria for oral genres. Consider this comment from anthropologist Lila Abu-Lughod:

> Bedouins are sensitive to the graces and evocative power of oral textual elements such as sound, alliteration, intonation, and rhythm…metaphors and new images…even familiar and ordinary images…derive great connotative richness from subliminal intertextual comparisons. Individuals know so many poems that each new one undoubtedly evokes image-traces and feeling-traces from others with shared words, phrases, or themes.

Yet they resist explicit analysis of their creations. The Bible, too, has complex literary nuances. Therefore, according to United Bible Society consultant William Smalley,

> *Translators must learn to use the subtlety, the indirection, the evocativeness, the imagery of the receptor language if they are to do justice to the Bible. (Although sometimes we) may have to reduce imagery to its ideational meaning and translate that the result is loss in interactional and textual power.*

Another UBS consultant, Jacob Loewen, studied West African praise poems to see if this genre could be used for some Old Testament poetry. He discovered that these poems "must have the rhythms of the drum tunes by which they are traditionally sung." Similarly cultivating connotations, ethnomusicologist Eugene Goudeau has paired traditional tunes with appropriate Christian events:

CURRENT TUNE ASSOCIATION	CHRISTIAN ADAPTATION
Welcome songs and songs announcing births	Christmas Baptism
General songs of joy	Resurrection
Puberty & initiation songs	Baptism
Wedding songs	Ordination
Victory songs	Christ's victory Christian's victory over sin
Coronation of chiefs	Crowning Christ Lord
Mourning songs	Holy communion, Lent

Connotations matter. Although poetry is not particularly important for Americans, in some countries it is so inflammatory that it has been banned from the radio. Poetic speech is an arena for profundity, where a multiplicity of meanings collide. We will never master it, but we can acknowledge its richness and keep learning, keep alert to the connotations. This will enhance the quality of our storytelling.

Action learning. Both Atkins and Irving get their students to teach. This is excellent. Storytelling is modeled, then roles are switched, and the listeners become the tellers. Feedback enhances the experience.

Other types of "action learning" might include drama, dance, liturgies, object lessons, field studies, and guided ministry apprenticeships. Both programs hint at such apprenticeships, but I would like to see these receive a higher profile, described in more detail, and presented as significant educational methods woven into the total curriculum (at least as significant as setting off a rocket in the jungle as part of a science course!).

Memorization. After Alberto murdered my relative, Mark, he couldn't get scripture out of his mind. It resonated in his head and eventually changed his life. In most of the world's religions, spiritual people memorize and recite. Irving's and Atkins' students memorize stories. I'd like them to expand this to verses and passages and even creeds and catechisms that roll off the tongue rhythmically.

There is a Pakistani community where 640 Muslims have come to faith over 30 years. Most have continued faithful. Memorization has been key. New believers have been required to learn 34 specific verses from the Gospel of John. Oral learners pick these up from other believers. As a result, they own the message. It is inside them. Some have become excellent evangelists.

This echoes the experience of God's people throughout history, whether the early Israelites, Wycliffe's "Poor Priests," or Christians jailed without Bibles today: the word in our hearts is alive. It reaches even to Alberto.

PERSPECTIVE III:

Andragogy and Approaches—Adult Learning and Oral Preference Learners

As we synthesize the previous section, we may be thinking: *How do we teach the "whole counsel" of God? Where does literacy get involved? How do we sensitize ourselves to the methodological approach of oral culture?*

Translating the previous section and the current Perspective into a larger global population of over 80 percent of oral preference learners is daunting for anyone.

What will it take for teachers/facilitators to engage and be effective where we are?

How do we teach, and which type of curriculum is appropriate for our audience?

Is there a place for evaluations?

What defines an oral theology which is wrong, and how do we handle it?

Moreover, *how do we fulfill the call of a teacher?*

How do we evaluate or test the learning of oral preference learners?

Or how can we respect older oral preference learners instead of deferring to younger learners who might prefer print-based learning?

How are we going to assess—know/be/do—and test the life change?

How do we adjust or modify and contextualize the role of the teacher without losing the authentic role of the teacher?

And conversely, how will the teachers embrace both the print and oral teaching methodologies?

Finally, *how does participatory learning fit in, and how does collaborative team-based learning become normative in adult learning approaches?*

Having completed 180 degrees, our Imagineering is heightened; to this, we are going to add another Perspective: andragogy. As you read this section with your colleagues, begin to think about how you will engage with the orality movement.

Chapter 8

Helping Adults Learn: Lessons from Andragogy and the Challenge of Context

LaNette W. Thompson

Malcolm Knowles noted in his book, *Andragogy in Action*, that although he had been the first to introduce the term "andragogy" into the literature of American adult education, he actually had stolen the term from the Europeans (1984, xvi).

As a young man working in a community job training program, he realized that some teachers were more effective in teaching adults than others. The effective teachers were supportive and helpful to their adult students, engaged them in participatory learning, were more informal with them, and treated them with respect (1984, 2-3).

As he began teaching and theorizing about issues in adult learning, a professor from Yugoslavia who attended one of Knowles' seminars introduced him to the European term "andragogy", the art and science of helping adults learn, as opposed to pedagogy, the art and science of teaching children (1984, 5-6). Knowles used the term and infused it with his own assumptions, which he refined over the years. Now, in the United States, even though the term can be traced in German literature back to the early nineteenth century, the term is associated with Knowles and his teachings (Cranton 1992, 13).

In this paper, I will examine Knowles' andragogical assumptions, consider characteristics of both Western and traditional West African educational practices, make suggestions for teaching in an oral context, and challenge us to examine our theological institutions in oral contexts.

In his book, Knowles describes seven elements of andragogical learning, most of which, such as the adults' need to formulate, design, carry out, and evaluate their own learning, have been criticized as more pertinent to independent Western cultures than the global arena of adult learning (Merriam, Caffarella, and Baumgartner 2007, 87-92). As we examine theological institutions in oral contexts, there is much we can learn, however, from Knowles' interpretation of the pedagogical and the andragogical models of education. Table 1 was constructed from Knowles' writings (1984, 8-12).

Assumptions about learners	Pedagogical Model of Education	Andragogical Model of Education
The learners' role in learning	Learners are submissive and dependent upon the teacher to make all decisions as to what is learned.	The learner is self-directed, actively seeking what needs to be learned.
The teachers' role in learning	Knowledge is transmitted though lectures, assignments, and media, with the focus on the teacher's experience and knowledge rather than the learners' experience.	Knowledge is discovered as individuals with quality life experiences and focused learning needs serve as resources to each other, learning through participatory educational activities. Teachers may assist students to appreciate others' views.

Learners' readiness to learn	Readiness is a function of age. Students become ready to learn when learning is necessary to pass to the next grade.	Learners become ready to learn when they have a need for knowledge or more effective performance in some area of their lives. Readiness occurs naturally as one passes through new life stages, but can also be encouraged by confronting learners with possibilities of betterment.
Learning orientation	Content-oriented learning; learning is seen as a process of acquiring knowledge. Curriculum is logically sequenced and organized according to content.	Problem, task, and/or life-centered approach to learning with learning content organized as it relates to life situations rather than subject matter.
Motivation for learning	Students motivated to learn in order to please others, avoid consequences from parents and teachers, get good grades, etc.	Occasionally motivated to please others as in job requirements, etc. Primary motivation is personal curiosity, desire for recognition, better quality of life, greater self-confidence, etc.

Contrary to his initial teachings that described pedagogy in opposition to andragogy, Knowles later came to describe the two models as parallel, admitting that in some situations children are self-directed learners and in some situations where adults are thrust into new territory, a pedagogical model of direct teacher-centered instruction may be best (1984, 12-13).

It is important not only to examine our institutional practices in light of whether they are more pedagogical or andragogical, but also to examine their historical context. In my book, *Sharing the Message Through Storying*, which was written for West African church leaders, I contrast Western and traditional West African educational practices, pointing out that many of the educational practices in the church resemble the Western educational models of those who instituted them.

In Western models, teachers are professionals with the ability to analyze their subject and give their own interpretations of the subject content. Such expertise requires time and money. Since teachers know more than their students, they are in positions of power and deserve a salary for sharing their specialized knowledge. Since the students are not experts, they are not expected to pass along what they have learned to others. Teachers must have a place to teach that is arranged according to the needs of the teacher. The students are dependent upon the teacher and the availability of books or other written resources. Starting new classes depends upon whether the teacher is available, if there is money to pay a salary, and a place that is conducive to teaching. Students' knowledge is assessed through written exams.

In the traditional West African model, which is primarily oral, teachers enter into relationships with their students. Often, the students are sent to live with the teachers.

Instruction, for the most part, is given according to the needs of the students and their ability to understand. Teaching is not limited to a particular time or day, but can occur in natural settings, often outdoors in mentor/apprentice relationships. Although the preferred teaching method is to use stories, teachers also use proverbs, games, and songs to pass along information and aid in the students' retention of information.

Students are expected to memorize important information, sometimes large blocks of information. Once the students understand the teaching, they put it into practice and are expected to teach what they have learned to younger learners. Teachers are not usually paid a salary, but receive gifts from the students' parents, or the students themselves might work for the teacher. The teacher in this model is revered and respected, having earned the right to teach through life experience. It is believed that the student learns as much from being in the presence of the teacher as by receiving particular instruction.

In examining how Jesus taught, it soon becomes obvious that Jesus' teaching methods more closely resemble the West African model than the Western one. Educational methods are highly influenced by our cultural values. One method is not necessarily the "right" method, especially if it ignores the needs of the majority of the population.

Some of Knowles' andragogical concepts, such as problem-centered learning and the need for adults to share from their experiences, are key elements in traditional oral education. Embedded in many Western concepts of adult learning, however, are Western cultural values that view the individual as an autonomous learner.

Research and theories of knowledge in the West assume that the body and mind are split—an assumption that impacts learning theory with a resulting emphasis on information processing, assessing intelligence, and cognitive development. Western communication is usually direct, with an emphasis on clarity. Some relational cultures which stress interdependence prefer indirect, subtle communication styles, sometimes even utilizing a third party if a message is especially important.

Cultural clashes occur in the classroom when Asian students who have been taught never to question teachers for fear of causing them to lose face attend American universities where they are expected to express their views openly (Merriam, Caffarella, and Baumgartner 2007, 218-224).

Tension can occur when administrators and professors in international theological institutions are from or were trained in an individualistic Western tradition and their students are from an oral, collectivist tradition. Likewise, when students are trained in the individualistic Western tradition but find they are unprepared for working among a primarily oral population, they become frustrated; even more significant, they can be ineffective in their ministries.

Based upon my experience teaching in West Africa, in my thesis, *The Nonliterate and the Transfer of Knowledge in West Africa*, I provided suggestions to westerners working in oral contexts (Thompson 1998, 29-32).

- The teacher must be humble and accessible. In many oral contexts, there is no inherent worth in the knowledge itself since knowledge is not separated from the giver of the knowledge. For the people to take the message seriously, the teacher's character must be above reproach as determined by the local context. Learning the local language will allow the teacher and student to communicate on a heart-to-heart level.
- Normal knowledge transfer is from older to younger. Young people serving as leaders should be encouraged to work either in subjection to an older adult in the community or in a close apprentice relationship with an older leader as Timothy was to Paul.
- Information should be put in context and long verbal discourses avoided. Stories, poetry, songs, chants, dance, theater, object lessons, and rituals facilitate learning.
- Learning and memorization of stories and biblical passages are important.
- The needs of the student take precedence over the needs of the teacher. Teaching sessions can be formal or informal, but should occur within the rhythm of the community if planting and harvest times are an issue.

One element of andragogy particularly helpful to our pursuit touches upon the psychological element of learning in a climate of mutual respect, collaboration, trust, support, openness, and authenticity (Knowles 1984, 15-16). This psychological element of treating adults as adults when they are the learners, rather than treating them like children, is a powerful concept, especially when literates are teaching oral people.

As theological education in oral contexts is examined, consider four possible teaching scenarios, each of which brings its own challenges.

- Literate adults from literate Western cultures who live in primarily oral cultures and teach literate as well as oral adults within that oral culture
- Literate adults from primarily oral cultures who have been trained or influenced by literate Western cultures, who teach both literate and oral adults within that oral culture
- Primarily oral adults from primarily oral cultures who teach oral adults but who also desire to use their limited literacy to learn from primarily literate adults
- Oral adults from primarily oral cultures who learn and teach by oral means

In most theological institutions, the last two scenarios (oral adults in positions of leadership teaching through oral means within the institution) are novel and perhaps frightening concepts. In many institutions, valued educational practices are in place which have been legitimized through time. These practices provide order and discipline to everyday life and are not changed easily. Some may even have difficulty appreciating learning "outside the traditional ethnocentric European paradigm" (Sparks and Butterwick 2004, 280-281).

As we look at the process of contextualizing theological education in oral contexts, we must first examine adult life and the societal context of the institution. Sharan Merriam, Rosemary Cafferella, and Lisa Baumgartner begin their book, *Learning in Adulthood*, with the statement, "…learning is a personal process—but a process that is shaped by the context of adult life and the society in which one lives" (2007, 1).

Are there societal values and educational practices that should be incorporated? Are current practices influenced by outdated historical Western influences? Would the needs of the students be better served by adjusting and adapting to more traditional oral methods with a contemporary twist? What current practices are worthwhile and need to remain? This examination and the resultant findings will differ from institution to institution.

As we ask these difficult questions, let us remember our mission and look foremost to scripture as our guide as we "lay aside every weight and the sin that so easily ensnares us, and run with endurance the race that lies before us, keeping our eyes on Jesus, the source and perfecter of our faith…" (Heb. 12:1-2).

Chapter 9

Important Lessons from Indigenous Movements and Locally-initiated Churches in the Global South

James R. Krabill

The Broader Picture of Religious Dynamism in Africa and Worldwide

There are at least 15,000 different denominations and new religious movements in sub-Saharan Africa today, most resulting from the encounter between African traditional religion(s) and Western Christianity.

The vast majority of these churches/movements are entirely local and indigenously African in polity, program, leadership, and finance. Between the various groups there exists an enormous spectrum of diversity in cultural, religious, and theological perspectives. Harold W. Turner was one of the first to identify different types of groups within this spectrum as "neo-primal", "synthetist", "Hebraist", "independent churches", and "mission-founded churches" (Turner 1967). Since Turner's writings, we have needed to add "evangelical/Pentecostal" churches to the mix (Krabill 2008, 64-70).

Religious understandings and practices among these groups range widely from movements only a step removed from traditional

African religious reality to faith communities focused on more Christ-centered, Spirit-led, biblically-oriented expressions of New Testament faith. While we are describing here the religious phenomenon on the African continent, it should be noted that the same reality exists worldwide wherever Western Christianity has encountered traditional, "primal" religions.

I am beginning my reflections here with this larger picture for several reasons:

1. Most Western Christian organizations continue to work in global settings with Western-founded/related churches and institutions. And these entities have not done particularly well at creatively working at the issue of ministry, training, and worship patterns in oral contexts, even though this remains an enormous challenge for institutions of Western origin. In a recent 759-page handbook on "theological education in world Christianity" (Werner 2010), with contributing authors from nearly every stream of the Christian family, there is virtually no reference to how the Church should be working at the monumental task of leadership training in oral settings.

2. Despite what Western Christians might think of the indigenous churches and movements that are borne of the encounter with Western Christianity, many are surviving and even thriving in oral contexts of ministry. Whether or not we agree on every point with their theological perspectives, they remain some of the best examples of what Western churches and Western-trained global leaders need to learn about this matter.

The Oral Character of Africa's Indigenous Church Reality

The life and worship experiences of indigenous churches/movements across sub-Saharan Africa are, for the most part, oral in character:

- **Paperless**—no bulletins, newsletters, hymnbooks, educational materials, brochures, few Bibles

- **Oral forms of communication**—preaching, congregational singing, choirs, shouts, prayers, prophesying, antiphonal/interactive-style of worship leading, inspired songs interrupting sermons
- **Full-body engagement**—hand clapping, pointing, dancing, kneeling, jumping, arm raising, prostrating, handkerchief waving, musical gestures, laying on of hands, turning in circles, facing in different directions
- **Spiritual gifts**—emphasis on speaking in tongues, interpreting dreams, song and prayer interventions, etc.
- **Important objects**—cross-staffs, baptismal bowls, worship attire, sprinkled water
- **Holy places**—arrangement of worship space, the "praying grounds," healing centers
- **Visual symbols**—dressing in white, seating assignments, leaders' vestments, community-building group-dancing in procession, sanctuary design and location, removing shoes, the use of specific colors in dress and décor, etc.
- **Contextualized practices and celebrations**—The "Flood Festival" (remembrance of God's promise to Noah at the end of the rainy season), use of cultural funeral rituals on Good Friday, pure coconut milk used in baptism, dancing the preacher (the "chief") in musical procession to and from church for every worship service, etc.

These are powerful pedagogical components in oral contexts that instruct the individual believer and the entire community on a number of important matters. They, in fact, affirm the following:

1. We do not have to be proficient in literacy to worship God.
2. God can speak to us in many ways in addition to the written word—through dreams, prophesies, etc. (There are dangers and risks in making statements like this, but the affirmation remains true nonetheless in oral-based communities.)
3. Faith is meant to be lived and experienced most fully in community.

4. The worship experience is enhanced when it becomes "multi-voiced" with active interaction between preacher, worship leader(s), and gathered assembly.

5. Worship is a whole-body, whole-life experience. Every part of our being as individuals and in corporate expression has been created and loved by God and should be offered back to him in thanksgiving and praise.

6. We remember best when we physically "do" something—remove our shoes, kneel in confession, etc.

7. Learning happens most deeply when all the senses—touch, taste, sounds, smells, and sights—are engaged.

8. Particular places, objects, colors, and rituals can point to deeper meanings and call us to a more mature faith through profound reflection, transformed attitudes, and changed behavior.

9. Worship is meant not only for the sanctuary, but also for the street.

10. Our local cultural patterns and practices can be adapted to our new life in Christ and used to build us up in the faith.

11. Biblical stories and celebrations can be translated into our time and place as "our story" becomes interwoven with "God's story."

The Specific Context of My Ministry

For almost two decades, from 1978-1996, I served as a Bible and church history teacher with Mennonite Board of Missions among some of these African-initiated churches across West Africa. A few of the leaders of these churches had elementary-school training and access to limited written materials. Most other church members did not.

The elderly preacher, N'Guessan Benoit, who ministered in the Ivorian village where our family lived for four years, had already been preaching for five decades when we arrived there in the early 1980s. Amazingly, "Papa" Benoit had no formal schooling and could understand but a very small percentage of the nineteenth-century archaic French-language Bible (the *Louis Segond* version) that he carried with him each week into the pulpit.

Wycliffe Bible translators had just arrived in the village at about the same time we did and had done little more than establish the alphabet in the local Dida language. So Louis Segond was unfortunately all that Benoit had. How, then, did this preacher manage to prepare sermons all those years and carry out his ministry of counseling the flock?

At the beginning of each week, Benoit would call into his courtyard a young elementary school lad, hand him his Bible, and tell him to pick a passage. Then, Benoit would say, "Now, read it to me." The young lad, himself with only a few years of French-language instruction, would do his best to bumble through.

"Now, tell me what it means," he would instruct. At this point, the young boy would attempt to take what he understood of the text and translate it into the Dida language—the medium Benoit would be using on Sunday morning to transmit God's word to the faithful. "Now do it again," Benoit would counsel, a second and third time. The old man listened to each rendition of the text with careful attentiveness and then committed it to memory for use during the upcoming week ... or on any future occasion when he might choose to recall it.

This was Papa Benoit's only access to scripture and the process he faithfully followed week after week during his lifetime of ministry. In 2011, at 100 years of age, Benoit went on to be with the Lord after a preaching career that had lasted eight decades.

Primary Teaching Approaches Applied in this Oral Context

Bible storying with a Luke 24 hermeneutic. It will not be surprising that biblical storytelling was an important feature in my teaching. But I struggled with which stories to tell and in what order. Most of my students had a rather "flat" view of scripture, with accounts of Solomon, Paul, Ruth, Moses, and Jesus available for plucking as one might choose random food items at a buffet.

Furthermore, the central hermeneutical principle Jesus taught his disciples on the road to Emmaus—i.e., "all of the Law and the prophets speak of me"—was generally missing from people's understanding. So rather than simply teaching our way through the story from Genesis to Revelation, we made Jesus the center focus for approaching and interpreting the biblical text. This was done through seeking to answer the following questions:

a. *Who was Jesus?* (Gospel of Mark in detail)
b. *Why did Jesus need to come into the world?* (Gen. 1-11)
c. *Who were Jesus' ancestors?* (Gen. 12—end of O.T.)
d. *What was Jesus' primary message?* (selections from Matthew, Luke, and John)
e. *Who were the people who believed and followed Jesus?* (Acts)
f. *What problems did they confront as a faith community gathered around Jesus?* (selections from the Epistles)
g. *What role does Jesus play in the future God is preparing?* (Revelation)

Dramatic productions designed for whole-village involvement. On several occasions, biblical dramas were created and produced by the Bible students. The performances took place at night on the village square with as many as 1,000 people in attendance—Christians, Muslims, and "traditionalists" alike. On one evening, the life of Elijah was presented with full dramatic effects, including fire from heaven when a student perched in a nearby tree poured a full can of gasoline on an open fire 20 ft. below (not my idea, but very impressive and enormously popular with the crowd!).

On another occasion, as a part of our Church History series, we presented a piece we called, "The early church—yesterday and today." In this drama, the students selected and acted out five scenes from the

Acts of the Apostles (conversions, power encounters, etc.), followed by five scenes from the life and ministry of William Wade Harris, the Liberian evangelist who was the first to present powerfully and effectively the gospel message to populations along the southern seaboard of the Ivory Coast. The presentation lasted for four hours. There were no microphones, pyro-technique special effects, or written script—just a mastery of the story, lots of on-the-spot improvisation, and plenty of passion and humor to make the stories come alive.

The use of hymns in historical reconstruction and theological reflection. Most of the indigenous churches we worked with composed their own music and other worship materials. The most impressive case was the movement that grew out of the ministry of William Harris referenced above. It is estimated that Harris baptized between 100,000-200,000 people during his 18-month tour in West Africa. He counseled new converts to return to their villages, to pray, preach, and compose songs in praise to God.

"God has no personal favorite songs," he told them. "God hears all that we sing in whatever language. It is sufficient for us to compose hymns of praise to him with our own music and in our own language for him to understand." Encouraged by these words of counsel the new believers set to work, transforming their traditional music into worship songs. The repertoire of hymns composed and sung by the Harrist Church today numbers in the thousands, all set to music by members of the church, for the church, and in a language that the church can well understand.

In one village where I taught, I took a hand-held recorder to church (seven services a week for almost four years) and collected over 500 original hymns, all composed over a 70-year period in that village. I was eventually able, through myriads of interviews, to date and classify these hymns in historical periods of composition.

This body of "faith statements set to music" became important in my teaching ministry. I used the songs in two primary ways:

- To help reconstruct the history of the Harrist movement through frequent references in the hymn texts to historical happenings that had never been written down and that very few people could otherwise still remember.
- To help the Bible students analyze specific terms and theological themes in the hymns to see what patterns emerged, how thought had changed over time, which parts of the Bible were most often referenced or neglected, and what important themes were misunderstood or totally ignored (see Krabill 1995).

Many people around the world have told me:

> We like sermons and we think they are an important part of worship. But when we get back to our homes, we often forget what was said. With songs, however, it is different. We sing them in our courtyards, while we bathe the children, at work in the fields. The melodies and rhythms help us remember the important lessons found in our hymns.

Couple these reflections with the following statement and we have a solid case for taking music more seriously as a pedagogical ally in cultures where orality reigns: "When a people develops its own hymns with both vernacular words and music, it is good evidence that Christianity has truly taken root" (Chenoweth and Bee 1968, 212).

Chapter 10

Orality Observations among Francophone West African Adults: Storying to Orality

Jeff Singerman

Orality, specifically storying, was introduced to IMB missionaries in West Africa in the early to mid-1990s. Theory and practical story sets were given to facilitate the implementation of storying as a strategy to reach the illiterate. It took years of repetitive storying trainings and testimonies shared from the few missionaries employing this strategy before it began to take hold among missionaries. Our Baptist partners were hesitant to embrace this approach primarily because it was a paradigm shift from the literate methodology that had been employed for years.

The strategy implemented was to bring several key Baptist leaders from all the West African countries together for one-week seminars in storying methodology. These leaders were chosen by missionaries to attend, circumventing the advice and input of Baptist partners. Primarily, time was spent on the theoretical approach of storying to convince partners of the method's effectiveness with limited modeling of storying methodology. The overall training was literate based. The Bible story was written in a book for the group leader to read and learn, followed by a series of printed questions to be asked of the participants once the story was presented. Storying, as presented in this manner, required reading ability. It was shackled to literate methodologies.

Missionaries desired that the attendees return to their home countries to implement storying on a wide scale. Unfortunately, this did not happen, in part because they did not fully understand the concept.

Even though some storying trainings were conducted in various countries to teach the core group, storying was never fully embraced by our Baptist partners.

In 2007, West African missionaries were trained in the oral participative Bible study model. Unfortunately, for the greater part of the training, literate methods were utilized to explain oral methodology. To their credit, much storytelling modeling was done with trainees being assigned stories in application of the principles.

After the three-week course, missionaries were once again requested to bring key African leaders to a central location so they could participate in this training methodology. Believing this a strategic mistake, I asked if my wife and I could instead travel to Francophone West Africa to reach people at the grassroots level. In their villages, we modeled orality with the participative Bible study, taught biblical truths, and mentored African trainers at the same time. Together, we transformed the orality presentation into a purely oral model.

A story set was developed with multiple dimensions:

1. To model oral methods and have each participant exercise the same
2. To convey a core biblical God-teaching: God's purpose (Dan. 2), God's promise (Acts 1-2), God's desire (Acts 10-11), God's strategy (John 4), and the key to accomplishing his vision being leaders training each member to do the work of the ministry (Acts 18, Eph. 4)

3. To enable each participant to realize the spiritual resources given him or her to accomplish God's task. These are: God's word (Matt. 4, temptation of Jesus), the Holy Spirit (Acts 8, Phillip), the gospel (Acts 16), prayer (Luke 11), and faith (Matt. 15, the Canaanite woman).

4. To empower all to witness

5. The necessity of obedience to God's word (Matt. 28:19-20) and holding each other accountable to steps of faith

Over the three-day training session, Creation to Church and the demoniac from Mark 5 were modeled. Each evening, participants promised to go and share the story and were expected to find someone, preferably not in attendance, with whom to share. The next morning, while emphasizing obedience and accountability, a testimony time ensued. The exuberance of many having won people to Christ was a great reinforcement of the effectiveness of using a story for witnessing.

After the initial storytelling, a willing participant from the audience was asked to stand up and repeat the story. Most often, someone was able to accomplish retelling the story accurately. At this point, a review phase was entered into to ensure that each had fully grasped the story. If the story was well understood, each person repeated the story to his or her neighbor. Usually a drama based upon the story was presented by the participants, for the participants. Their grasp and cultural adaptation of the stories were compelling. Only after these components had been completed did the participative Bible study begin.

Four open-ended questions were asked after each story: *What lessons have you learned from this story? What characteristics of God are portrayed in the story? What have you learned in this story that you need to obey starting today? To whom will you tell the story?* The insights they gained through God's stories were astounding. No teaching on our part was necessary. God's remarkable Spirit revealed truth to them.

The danger we encountered was participants trying to explain the unexplainable by going outside the context of the story to develop a spiritual theory of "why" certain things happened a certain way. We would continually shift them back to theological soundness by saying, "God didn't answer that question, therefore, it is not a question he intended to answer before eternity." The story session generally concluded with a song, preferably one that corresponded with the story, and dance.

During one of our initial training events, after the presentation of Creation to Church as a witnessing tool, many in the audience began to ask what should be included in this type of story. They realized that many aspects of the story could be tailor-made depending upon the target audience. I took a piece of chalk and went to the blackboard to list various suggestions of what could be included.

Suddenly, the whole atmosphere of the training turned negative. What had begun in true participation of all being equal now turned to emphasizing the literate, as I listed things to go into the story. Communication broke down. After a few moments I realized what I had done and the dramatic change that had taken place. From that moment on I never again wrote anything down or gave out any literature until after the training was finished.

For those who desired it, once the training was over, we provided story sets and handouts on what we had discussed during the training period. We did this believing that it might help those who were literate to continue. However, from the start to finish of orality training, we held no piece of paper, never once wrote anything on a blackboard, or used any type of handouts during the training so as to totally model an oral methodology of training and participative Bible study. All participants, both literate and illiterate, were able to visualize how this training could be implemented at all levels of church life.

A particularly difficult part of the process was to compel them to envision present and future implementation of oral methodology in their church situations, to create "action plans." After trial and error God led us to dramatize a discussion between two church leaders talking through the principles that had been taught and how the methodology could be incorporated into church life. This helped convey that we were looking for immediate planning by each person and church present. To be able to hold them accountable, we required someone in the group to write their plans in French or a local language, which reverted the process to literate methods. The drama conveyed the purpose and plan; nevertheless, we are still perplexed as to how to achieve this in a purely oral manner.

In the training sessions, not reviewing the story and immediately asking the participative questions was not helpful. We found that the story being told, reviewed once at a minimum, and then being told again by each of the participants to his or her neighbor, gave an adequate understanding of all the elements of the story that was presented. We experimented with shortening this process by eliminating one of the above steps, but inaccuracies when retelling the story abounded. Participants needed to listen, review, and repeat the stories for them to be fully understood and embraced.

Teaching oral methodologies in a purely academic, theoretical setting may be good for laying a foundation for the training of trainers. Some African leaders have expressed to us their desire for this type of documentation and theoretical guidelines. However, the concrete thinking of most West Africans' teaching and modeling from a thoroughly oral perspective seems to be the key for conveying the concept of orality. Everyone, no matter their level of education, quickly grasped the methodology and all were equally able to respond and catch a vision for how this methodology could be used in all aspects of church life.

We plan to continue oral training and teaching with the grassroots associations and will cover pertinent issues addressing the needs of that particular area. We will craft stories to be used in addressing spiritual warfare, the Christian family, leadership, etc. We desire to continue to model orality, train trainers, and analyze and evaluate its effectiveness, as well as to answer questions from those who are applying oral principles in all aspects of the church.

Theological Education

Theological training in West Africa began with theological education by extension. Gradually, Bible schools and seminaries were established, which catered to only one small segment of the population, the literate.

In 2002, the Benin Baptist Convention, on their own initiative, began a traditional Bible school. About the same time, they started a pilot oral theological Bible school in the Fon language. Since its founding, they have had two oral Bible school graduating classes. Recently, the school has opened two satellite campuses among the Maxi and Yoruba people groups. Typically, students gather for one week each month to memorize ten Bible stories and discuss doctrine and theology that are contained within each. They learn 150 Bible stories over a three-year period.

I hope to look at this oral model and compare it with those going through the traditional approach to theological education. All aspects of the training will be examined as to their outcome. Professors, as well as graduates from the traditional and oral Bible schools, will be interviewed as well as the churches in which the students serve. My goal is to qualify and quantify the "product" from both aspects of training done in the same school. My desire is to make this a viable model for other West African countries so that they may have both approaches to theological education.

We must explore creative options with existing Bible schools and seminaries to give "accreditation" and proper recognition to those who have completed an oral theological training. This will be easier to accomplish among younger or less established conventions than among those who have had theological schools and ecclesiastical guidelines in place for decades. Some of our IMB missionaries who teach in a literate seminary are using oral methodologies when possible in their classrooms.

This is helping break down barriers that still exist between literate and oral-based methodologies. We must seek ways to strategize together with partners on how best to reach oral-preference learners.

Questions to Explore

How can we implement the creation of long-term goals and strategies that will satisfy those of us from the West but will also be helpful to our partners? Is there a creative way to do this in a non-literate method? We must not lose sight of the necessity of traditional theological education and should not minimize its importance. We should strive for balance in using both methodologies. *How can we better train Majority World theologians in oral methodologies so that they can effectively implement and monitor progress in oral Bible schools?*

Chapter 11

A Response to the Articles in Perspective III

Steve Evans

*A man was running, stumbling, and gasping for breath as a ferocious tiger chased him. Dashing for the edge of a cliff, he saw a vine. He desperately reached for the vine and in one last, bold leap swung himself over the cliff's edge. As he hung dangling down, he looked up and saw the growling tiger on the ledge above him. He felt a moment of relief as the tiger clawed the air but was unable to reach him. Then the man looked down. At the bottom of the cliff far below where he hung was **another** tiger. Tightening his hold on the vine, the man wondered what to do. To his further dismay, he noticed two mice, one dark as night, one light as day, nibbling at the vine. He knew that it was only a matter of time before he would fall to the jaws of the tiger below. Just then, he noticed a wild strawberry growing on the face of the cliff. Gripping the vine with one hand, he reached out with the other, plucked the strawberry from the cliff wall, and put it in his mouth. Never before had he realized how sweet a strawberry could taste (Forest 1996, 40).*

I feel a bit like the man in this popular Zen tale: the tiger above representing the three authors of the papers to which I am responding; the tiger below representing members of the theological and orality academia I am addressing. The only consolation is the topic at hand—theological education for adults of oral cultures, a topic as sweet to us as the strawberry is in the story!

When I took on this assignment to respond to the three papers, I immediately did three things: (1) I looked up the word "andragogy", (2) I went to the papers and looked for stories, and (3) I checked to see if the papers clearly represented the task each was assigned.

The word *andragogy* is not one I frequently use (in fact, I must confess, this is the first time in my life that I *have* used it), and I have learned that it means *adult* education vs. the *childhood* education of pedagogy. For me, the topic of discussion became much clearer: theological education for adult learners of oral cultures.

When I went to the papers (written by some of our best practitioners who really know orality), I unfortunately saw they were short on stories, but long on lists, points, sub-points, and bullet points—a big taboo in the field of orality as I understand it. Noting a lack of stories in these papers is *my* bias, however, and not one necessarily embraced by all those participating in this gathering. And I do recognize that this is an academic meeting and some level of academic-speak (and writing) is accepted, and even expected, here. So grace must prevail!

My colleagues and I were asked to address the following topic: theological education from the andragogical perspective of the adult oral learner and/or leader. LaNette Thompson, assigned the topic of learning methods, presented the paper "Helping Adults Learn: Lessons from Andragogy and the Challenge of Context." Dr. James Krabill, assigned the topic of global music ethnology and oral learners, presented the paper "Important Lessons from Indigenous Movements and Locally-Initiated Churches in the Global South." Finally, Jeff Singerman, assigned the topic of comparative experiences among several oral learning communities in Africa, presented the paper "Orality Observations among Francophone West African Adults."

A Response to Helping Adults Learn: Lessons from Andragogy and the Challenge of Context

LaNette Thompson does a wonderful job in presenting Knowles' andragogical assumptions, contrasting them with Western, West African, and pedagogical characteristics. It may be helpful to have a clear, concise definition and description of the term *andragogy*. Simply put, andragogy is the scholarly approach to the life-long learning of adults that incorporates both theory and practice.

According to Knowles, adults need to know the reason for learning. It needs to be experiential and they need to be included in the education process. There must be relevance and immediate application and it is usually problem-centered and internally motivated (http://www.instructionaldesign.org/theories/andragogy.html). It is interesting to note that there are current studies going on in the area of adult education and problem solving. One of those by the Skillshare Challenge, StorySolving, is a methodology that combines storytelling, process drama, and tough topics in order to teach positive problem solving (http://skillshare.maker.good.is/projects/storysolving). (We should also take note of Stephen Denning and the use of storytelling in corporate cultures as a method of implementing the principles of orality in any andragogical setting, not just Bible storying since narrative theory and practice spans a much larger scope than Bible storying.)

There appear to be many parallels, in particular, between Knowles's description of adult learning styles and Thompson's description of West African learning styles. Her statement, "It is believed that the student learns as much from being in the presence of the teacher as by receiving particular instruction," clearly shows the significance of the relational-experiential aspect of education expressed by Knowles.

Thompson makes a brief reference to the teaching methodologies of Jesus, but offers no details. The relevance seems vital, however, since our topic at hand is adult learning and theological education. Jesus and his disciples fit the bill perfectly! May I offer the following?

The Wise Man (Matt. 7)

Jesus spent time with his disciples. He walked with them, ate with them, slept with them, and even told them stories. One day, when Jesus saw the crowds of people who sought him out, he went up on a mountainside, sat down with his disciples, and began to teach them. When he was nearly finished, he said:

"These things that I say to you are not incidental; they are foundational. They are words to build a life on. If you let them enter your life, you are like a wise man who built his house on solid rock. Rain poured down, the waters rose, and the wind blew, but the house stood firm. Everyone who hears these words of mine, but doesn't act on them—doesn't work them into their lives and apply them—is like the foolish man who built his house upon the sand. The rains poured down, the waters came up, the wind blew—all fiercely crashing against the house—and the house totally collapsed."

When Jesus finished with these words, the crowds were amazed at his teaching, because he taught them as one having authority.

The Sower, the Seed, and the Soils (Mark 4)

So it is that whenever Jesus taught, he used stories and parables. One day the crowds that followed Jesus got so big that he got into a boat and pushed out into the water while the crowds remained on the shore. Using stories and parables, he began teaching them many things. He said:

"Listen! A farmer went out and planted seed. Some of it fell on the roadside and the birds ate it. Some fell on

rocky ground, where there was not much dirt. It sprouted up quickly, but didn't put roots down very deep. The sun scorched it, and it withered away. Some seed fell among weeds and thorns, and the weeds and thorns choked it, and it didn't produce fruit. But some seed fell on good soil, and it sprang up and grew and produced good fruit—even beyond expectations!"

"Listen to this," Jesus said. "Are you listening? Really listening?"

When they were by themselves, those who were close to him, along with his twelve disciples, asked Jesus about the story. He told them, "You've been given insight into God's kingdom—you know how it works. But to those who can't see it yet, everything comes in stories, making them ready and receptive, nudging them toward insight." Then Jesus said, "You don't know this story? You don't understand it? Then how will you know, how will you understand, any of my stories?" Jesus then explained the story of the Sower, the Soils, and the Seed to those around him. He said:

"The farmer sows the Word. Some people are seed that falls on the roadside. Immediately after they hear, Satan comes and snatches away what has been planted in them. Some are like the seed that lands in the rocky ground. When they first hear the Word, they receive it with gladness. They only last a short time, though, and when the emotions wear off and some difficulty arrives, there is nothing to show for it. The seed sown in the weeds and thorns represents the ones who hear the word, but the cares of the world and the deceitfulness of riches and desires for other things, choke out the word and nothing comes of it. But the seed planted in the good soil represents those who hear the Word, embrace it, and produce a harvest way beyond their expectations." Jesus then shared several other parables and stories about the Kingdom of God.

> *With many stories like these, Jesus spoke to the*
> *people, sharing the Word with them, presenting his message*
> *to them, but only as much as they were able to hear it and*
> *receive it. He was never without a story when he spoke,*
> *and when he was alone with his disciples; he went over*
> *everything, explaining what the stories meant.*

"In examining how Jesus taught, it soon becomes obvious that Jesus' teaching methods more closely resemble the West African model than the Western one," Thompson says. "Educational methods are highly influenced by our cultural values. One method is not necessarily the 'right' method, especially if it ignores the needs of the majority of the population." This is a valid point that is supported by Knowles' interpretation of the pedagogical and andragogical models of education.

One further note to make on the teaching methods of Jesus comes from his encounter with unbelieving leaders. He concludes by telling them, "I did not speak of my own accord, but the Father who sent me commanded me **what** to say and **how** to say it" (John 13:49, emphasis mine). This "how to say" the truth comes through at dinner with Simon, the Pharisee:

> *At a by-invitation-only dinner a woman with a*
> *sordid past came from behind Jesus as he reclined at the*
> *meal, and with tears streaming off her face onto his feet she*
> *even anointed his feet with an expensive perfume. Simon,*
> *and all his self-righteous guests thought to themselves, "This*
> *is no prophet! He doesn't even know the shady character of*
> *this woman enough to disassociate himself from her."*
> *Jesus then said, "Simon, I have something to tell you."*
> *[What to say.] He then proceeded to tell a story about some*
> *men in debt to the moneylenders that they could not pay back.*
> *One owed a huge amount; the other a small amount, and the*
> *man cancelled both their debts. Next, Jesus asked a question:*
> *"Which debtor loved the creditor more?" To which Simon*

answered, "I suppose the one who had the bigger debt."

Jesus opened Simon to the truth: "While you neglected to show me basic Jewish hospitality, this woman understood who I am and has done nothing but make me the center of her attention, because she knows she needs forgiveness more than anything. I tell you, her many sins have been forgiven because she loved much."

Finally, to Simon Jesus puts it in a proverb [how to say it] and an application: "He who has been forgiven little, loves little." To the woman he says, "Your sins are forgiven. Your faith has saved you; go in peace [Shalom]."

A Response to Important Lessons from Indigenous Movements and Locally-initiated Churches in the Global South

James Krabill's descriptions of components in oral contexts that instruct and inform believers individually and in community on the expression of worship are, as he says, both powerful and rich. While he calls these pedagogical components (which I'm positive are andragogical as well), Krabill goes well beyond his assigned topic of andragogy, ethnomusicology, and theological education, and takes us into the whole realm of experiential worship. He introduces us to the oral characteristics of the African indigenous church movement and gives us a glimpse of the life of the Church in that setting, adding applications of the characteristics to theological education and the adult oral learner.

Krabill should be commended for his desire to speak into "the issues of ministry, training, and worship patterns in the oral context." Referring to Warner's 759-page *Theological Education in World Christianity*, he says, "There is virtually *no* reference to how the church should be working at the monumental task of leadership training in oral settings." This is, indeed, a sad state of affairs and only emphasizes the need for meetings and presentations such as these. Pointing to indigenous church movements, Krabill says:

Despite what Western Christians might think of the indigenous churches and movements that are borne of the encounter with Western Christianity, many of them are surviving and even thriving in oral contexts of ministry. Whether or not we agree on every point with their theological perspectives, they remain some of the best examples of what Western churches and Western-trained global leaders need to learn about this matter.

Krabill's three teaching approaches applied to oral contexts are insightful: Bible storying, drama, and indigenous hymnody. They beg for even further examples to bring them to life! In fact, Krabill's entire presentation screams for more narrative examples. It is so rich in content that we want to savor it slowly through varied illustrative content.

Krabill's emphasis on the experiential, a key component to adult education according to Knowles, is excellent. The following story comes to mind, taken from Vincent Donovan's classic book, *Christianity Rediscovered.*

The Lion Is God

I used to think that faith was a head trip, a kind of intellectual assent to the truths and doctrines of our religion. I know better. When my faith began to be shattered, I did not hurt in my head. I hurt all over.

Months later when all this passed, I was sitting talking to a Masai elder about the agony of belief and unbelief. He used two languages to respond to me—his and Kiswahili. He pointed out that the word my Masai catechist, Paul, and I used to convey faith was not a very satisfactory word in their language. It meant literally "to agree to." I, myself, knew the word had that shortcoming. He said to believe like that was similar to a white hunter shooting an animal with his gun from a great distance. Only his eyes and fingers took part in the act. We should find another word.

He said for a man really to believe is like a lion going after its prey. His nose and eyes and ears pick up the prey. His legs give him the speed to catch it. All the power of his body is involved in the terrible death leap and single blow to the neck with the front paw, the blow that actually kills. And as the animal goes down the lion envelopes it in his arms (Africans refer to the front legs of an animal as its arms), pulls it into himself, and makes it part of himself. This is the way a lion kills. This is the way a man believes. This is what faith is.

I looked at the elder in silence and amazement. Faith understood like that would explain why, when my own was gone, I ached in every fiber of my being. But my wise old teacher was not finished yet.

"We did not search for you, Padri," he said to me. "We did not even want you to come to us. You searched us out. You followed us away from your house into the bush, into the plains, into the steppes where our cattle are, into the hills where we take our cattle for water, into our villages, into our homes. You told us of the High God, how we must search for him, leave our land and our people to find him. But we have not done this. We have not left our land. We have not searched for him. He has searched for us. He has searched us out and found us. All the time we think we are the lion. In the end, the lion is God." (Donovan 1978, 48)

The lion is God. That is theology in the context of an oral indigenous culture. Whether we agree with the theology of it or not, it clearly illustrates the experiential component of adult theological education for the adult oral learner.

A Response to Orality Observations among Francophone West African Adults Storying to Orality

Jeff Singerman does an excellent job in describing processes for the development of a Bible storying strategy, selecting a set of Bible stories for use in the strategy, story development and crafting, and evaluating the effectiveness of such a strategy. His presentation is full of personal experiences and insights, and his warning of using literate-based training "shackled to literate methodologies" is important. He explains the consequences of a mis-step during one training he conducted:

> *I took a piece of chalk and went to the blackboard to list various suggestions of what could be included. Suddenly, the whole atmosphere of the training turned negative. What began in true participation of all being equal, now turned to emphasizing the literate, as I listed things to go into the story. Communication broke down. After a few moments I realized what I had done and the dramatic change that had taken place. From that moment on I never again wrote anything down or gave out any literature until after the training was totally finished.*

Singerman clearly comes to the conclusion that oral teaching methods for oral cultures are the key to successful theological education for adults of those cultures.

Singerman's description of an oral theological Bible school for Fon speakers of Benin is extremely valuable. His conclusion that theological education in oral cultures should be taken to the people instead is commendable. Such models need to be written up as case studies to be shared among those involved in formalized theological education in oral contexts. I strongly encourage Singerman to follow up on his desire to create such a study, comparing this methodology to our standard traditional approaches to theological education.

Conclusions

How is the idea of theology in an oral context derived? *Strength* is a West African Limba tale that is endearing, sobering, and thought-provoking.

Strength

One day, elephant had the idea to have a contest to see who was the strongest. Chimpanzee tied a small tree in a knot. Deer ran three miles into the forest and three miles back. Leopard mightily scraped the ground with his powerful claws. Bushbuck plowed a road through the cane-fields with his horns. Elephant brought down a huge tree. With each feat, all declared that, indeed, it was a show of strength. Then it was man's turn. He whirled, twirled, did somersaults and cartwheels. "That's not strength," the animals said. Man climbed a tree and threw down the palm nuts. "That's great, but not strength," the animals said again. Then man took a gun and shot elephant dead.

Man was jumping and bragging.
"Strength! Strength!
"Wasn't THAT strength?
"Strength…"
Man looked around.
The animals were gone.
They had fled into the forest.
"Strength!…"
There was no one left to hear him brag.
Man was alone.

In the forest the animals huddled together and talked.
"Did you see that?"
"Was that strength?"
"Would you call that strength?"
"No. That was DEATH."
"That was DEATH."

Since that day the animals will not walk with Man.
When Man enters the forest he has to walk by himself.
The animals still talk of Man…
*That creature **Man**…*

He is the one who cannot tell the difference
between strength
and death.

Theology for the adult learner in oral contexts is experiential, whether through real-life experiences or through stories heard. From the teachings of Jesus, to the wisdom of a Masai elder, to traditional tales from around the world, we see that the adult learner hears it, walks with it, talks it, eats with it, and lives it. Conclusions, deductions, and applications are made that become part of the participant's worldview, values, beliefs, and practices. The observations and conclusions of Thompson, Krabill, and Singerman have merely cracked open the door to a world of learning characteristics of adult theological education in oral contexts that needs to be fully explored and put into practice.

PERSPECTIVE IV:

Affirming and Empowering—The Oral Preference Learner and the Oral Leader

In the previous Perspective, we were confronted with some effective means of assessment. *How do we really teach—is it through lecturing or "evoking"? Is there a way that we can have synthesis between individual and group learning (synergogy)? What is a biblical model for discipleship? Beyond information transfer is there a successful transformation?*

We are confronted with what exactly do we assess in the "know/ be/do" process? And how do we test life change?

We are on our last Perspective and a completion towards a 360-degree horizontal view focusing on oral preference learners and leaders. Clearly, we are sensing a disturbance! We are keenly aware that orality is requiring a multidisciplinary approach to training. Our Imagineering has also shaped our thinking. We ask loudly:

How can we affirm oral preference learners?

What are we going to do to empower our music composer theologians and those of the other arts?

How many oral preference students can a single print-based professor really evaluate or mentor?

As you approach this last section, seek to answer the following questions:

How might you collaborate with oral leaders?

How might your role, classroom, church, office, business, organization, or domain accommodate oral preference learners?

For any assessment process, how might you co-op input from oral leaders?

Chapter 12

Teaching Oral Learners in Institutional Settings

W. Jay Moon

Painting a Picture

Dipping his brushes into bright shades of turquoise, teal, and crimson, the artist splashes images on the canvas. Stepping back to view the resulting painting, clear patterns emerge.

To paint a picture of an oral learner, this article uses three institutional settings for brushes: an American seminary, a Native American reservation, and a rural African village. While these institutions are miles apart, the broad brushstrokes paint a coherent picture. The artist's palette is filled with these colors in the oral learners' world: dialogue, oral art, experience, holism, mnemonics, and participation. Stepping back to look at the painting, this article suggests approaches for teaching oral learners in institutional settings.

American Seminary (Moon 2012a)

The shuffle of notebook paper, furrowed brows, and unsteady hands signaled the arrival of the dreaded day; the assignment was due. This assignment could be turned in two ways: through a written assignment or an oral presentation. David, a bright and hard-working seminary student, made his way to the front of the room to turn in his written work. As I read over it, it was unclear whether he thoroughly understood and applied the material. Based upon the grading rubric for written assignments, he earned a "C" grade.

When David made his way to the front of the room to speak, there was confusion in the room. David had misunderstood the directions and incorrectly assumed that a paper and oral presentation were both necessary; therefore, he proceeded to give his oral presentation to the class. This time, he clearly articulated an understanding of the material, followed by an insightful discussion and creative application involving the other students. Using the oral presentation grading rubric, he earned an "A" grade. His vibrant expressions and deep understanding of the material was fully articulated orally.

Native American Reservation

John, a Native American, was a bright and promising student. One day, he emailed me to describe how the written approach slowed down his learning. Instead of starting with abstract theories and then trying to apply them, he preferred to be immersed in experiences that were connected to real events, people, and struggles of life. This connection then enabled him to connect theory to interpret his experiences. The formal analytical dissection and then reconstruction seemed too abstract, and they removed him from the context.

"Come visit and I will show you how we learn best," he explained. I took him up on his offer. When I arrived, the students joined in a local Pow-wow. A young dancer entered the center of the circle, wearing eagle feathers extended from his headdress up to the sky. Beautiful beadwork covered his moccasins from his toes up to his knees, as the dancer glided inside the circle. The beaded breastplate moved up and down as the shaker in his hand kept time with the beat.

Amidst the dancing, he leaned over and said, "Native Americans dance their prayers." A sweat lodge ceremony followed the dance, a symbol of purification and cleansing. That night, John led a discussion about contextual theology, utilizing oral literature to conceptualize it. All of the dancing, symbols, and rituals were recalled as he described a biblical understanding of Christ in culture.

Village in West Africa (Moon 2012b)

By the light of the kerosene lantern, villagers gathered in the mud-walled church to learn theology. As a young missionary, I was eager to meet with new believers to teach translated Bible studies that focused on important biblical topics like sin, salvation, and assurance. Confused looks, furrowed brows, and droopy eyes revealed that these topical studies were hard for people to grasp in the context of their culture.

Feeling he was losing them, George, the African pastor, applied oral learning approaches by using local proverbs to connect the disciples' thinking and memory patterns. George used the proverb Yaapta daa kpaalim, wuuta ale nam (When the elephants fight, the grass suffers) to describe how suffering results when leaders are not in agreement. George connected this with the concept that suffering is a result of the ongoing battle between God and Satan. He also composed songs and used local stories, charged with audience participation. Laughter filled the room and disciples were becoming transformed. Eventually, these students enacted some of the stories in contextualized dramas to the delight of others encircling them.

Oral vs. Print Educational Approaches

These three institutional settings highlight oral educational approaches. While the contexts are different, they have many similarities. Previous generations assumed that print methods were the most effective for education, but instructors are discovering oral learning patterns have the power to transform people into the image of Christ. Best of all, perhaps, instructors recognize that God has already placed these oral genres in culture, and they are useful for "teaching them to obey all that I have commanded you" (Matt. 28).

While other sources (Ong 1982, Lovejoy 2007, Moon 2009, Moon 2010) describe this more broadly, Table 1 highlights pedagogical differences between oral and print learners:

Table 1. Oral vs. Print Learning Preferences

Category	Oral Learners' Preference	Print Learners' Preference
Dialogue	Learn mostly in dialogue with others, often communicate in groups	Learn mostly alone, often communicate one to one
Oral Art	Appreciate clarity/style of speech through oral art forms (e.g., stories, proverbs, songs, dance, drama)	Appreciate clarity/validity of reasoning through interesting literature
Experience	Learn best when teaching is connected to real events, people, and struggles of life	Learn by examining, analyzing, comparing, and classifying principles that are removed from actual people and struggles (events are examples)
Holism	View matters in the totality of their context, including everyone involved (holistically)	View matters abstractly and analytically (compartmentally)
Mnemonics	Mnemonic devices like stories, symbols, songs, rituals, repetition serve as valuable memory aids	Written words can be recalled later; therefore, value brevity and being concise. Stories merely help illustrate points
Participation	Respond to a speaker and participate in a storytelling event	Listen quietly to the speaker and read alone

Suggestions from Oral Learners to Educators

The following suggestions are meant to help educators understand oral learners and then utilize this learning preference to facilitate student learning and transformation.

1. **Assessment**. First of all, use the Orality Assessment Tool to assess your own learning preference (Abney 2010), because you are likely using teaching and evaluation methods based upon your own learning preference. For instance, if you are a print learner, then you may be connecting well with other print learners, while not connecting with the oral learners. Even worse, you may be evaluating students based upon your own learning preference instead of their mastery of the material. This may lead to some false conclusions about the students' intelligence and comprehension of material.

2. **Dialogue**. Since oral learners often learn best in dialogue with others, create opportunities for dialogue to occur. This could be in the form of group projects outside of class or small group discussions in the classroom. During a class discussion on a difficult topic one day, a highly oral student presented a metaphor to the class that perfectly fit the situation and helped many other students to get the point. The class was amazed at the accuracy and relevance of the metaphor.

   David, a highly oral student, was also amazed as he exclaimed, "I have never thought of that metaphor before, and I would have never thought of it by reading and reflecting by myself. It is only during this dialogue that this came to me for the first time." Oral learners often appreciate and learn best through dialogue with others; therefore, it is important to foster opportunities for this to occur.

3. **Oral art**. Oral learners often express themselves through "oral art" instead of written words. How it is said is just as important as what is said. In place of a final paper, some students submitted video presentations about homelessness and poverty. They visited people on the street, interacted

with them, and interviewed them. The final video was very engaging, informative, and an effective use of the field research methods discussed in class.

In another class, students were encouraged to express their understanding and application of the class material through a simulation they designed for class participation. The simulations were highly creative and engaged the entire class in participatory learning. Terry, an oral student, responded afterward, "Finally, someone is teaching in the way we like to learn."

Keep in mind that visual art is also an aspect of orality. Smith (2006, 2) reminds us, "Visual illustrations are some of the first and oldest communication methods predating language... Oral people are very visually oriented." Professors should encourage creative expressions beyond written papers so that oral learners can express themselves better. For example, one oral learner submitted a collage instead of a term paper. The collage expressed all of the main themes of the class and she was able to articulate her understanding through her artwork. In an increasingly image-rich globalizing world, this area of orality (oral and visual art) will likely gain importance in education.

4. **Experience**. Oral learners also learn best when learning is connected to real events, people, and struggles of life instead of learning principles that are removed from actual people and struggles. Students appreciate it when professors arrange for these experiences to occur. A visit to the Native American reservation engaged students with a traditional medicine man, government officials, behavioral health workers, community development workers, pastors, etc. The students returned to the classroom energized to seek answers to their personal experiences.

    Immersion experiences like this help oral students in particular, since they begin with their experiences and realities of life. Eventually they develop questions, which then lead them to theories for explanation. Print learners, on the other hand, tend to prefer learning the theories first, and then seek to apply them to the realities of life. By arranging immersion experiences up front, oral learners are engaged in the learning process such that they are then eager to learn the theories that apply to their experiences.

5. **Holism**. Whereas print learners prefer to analyze, dissect, and compartmentalize abstract principles in learning (e.g., the three-point sermon), oral learners prefer to view matters in the totality of their context, including everyone involved (holistically). For example, oral learners often prefer to learn from the "whole to the part." Professors can help oral learners by explaining the overall context of an individual learning exercise so that he or she can see how this fits into the overall course. Mark Bauerlein (2008) made the following observation in class,

> *In an Introduction to Poetry class awhile back, when I asked students to memorize 20 lines of verse and recite them to the others at the next meeting, a voice blurted, "Why?" The student wasn't being impudent or sullen. She just didn't see any purpose or value in the task. Canny and quick, she judged the plodding process of recording others' words a primitive exercise. "Besides, if you can call up the verse any time with a click, why remember it?" she asked.*

Bauerlein then infers that student intelligence is declining. While Bauerlein's explanation is possible, another explanation is that this intelligent student was an oral learner who was striving to understand the larger context that would give meaning to this individual assignment. If the context was explained and she understood how this individual piece fit into the larger whole, then her learning would be greatly aided.

6. **Mnemonics**. Primary oral cultures have developed mnemonic teaching devices over many years that greatly facilitate the learning process. Oral learners appreciate professors who recognize and employ these mnemonic devices. Vivid mental pictures in stories, for example, are wonderful containers of wisdom for students to carry home and remember for an extended amount of time. Earthy proverbs and drama re-enactments can take words and put them on their feet. Rituals or ceremonies where the oral learner participates also help drive meaning deeper.

In a class discussion on symbols and ceremonies, we borrowed a chief installation ceremony from Africa and adapted it in the classroom for a professor installation ceremony. Each student participated in the construction and enactment of the ceremony, and he or she brought symbols to the class to communicate meanings that are hard to express by words alone. Following the ceremony, the class commitment, unity, and participation greatly increased, particularly among the oral learners. Their understanding of how symbols operate in ceremonies also greatly increased.

In addition, songs are an effective tool to help students with memory recall. In a class discussion on the abstract topic of epistemology, I played a few popular songs in class and asked the students to identify the underlying epistemology. After they sat and enjoyed the songs, they were then eager to understand, discuss, and see the relevance of the topic. Furthermore, the oral learners were able to remember the lesson in future classes.

7. **Participation**. While print learners prefer to read alone and listen quietly, oral learners prefer to respond to a speaker and participate in a storytelling event. In churches with oral audiences, there is often more audience participation. The preacher relies upon the congregation to help raise the energy and create an experience.

"Can I hear an Amen?" says the preacher to an oral audience, and the congregation responds. If there is no reaction, the preacher may reply, "Don't leave me up here by myself!" upon which the audience is reminded to participate.

In the classroom, oral learners will appreciate the opportunity to participate with the professor and other students. Simulation exercises help oral learners participate in the learning process. When discussing cross-cultural communication, a simulation divided the class into two different "cultures" to drive home the obstacles and potential strategies for overcoming cross-cultural misunderstandings. While print learners may see this as a waste of time since they want to learn and write down the principles, oral students tend to enjoy these simulations, reflect on them, and remember the meaning long afterward.

Summary

David, an African trained in an American seminary, continued to struggle using print learning preferences but excelled under oral learning preferences. John completed his doctoral studies but still prefers oral methods as he conducts courses on the reservation, immersing his "brush" in oral learning approaches. George became a popular speaker and pastor, as his teaching was well received, easily processed, and readily remembered.

Dipping into well-known cultural patterns, these three brushes portray a picture worth keeping. Using oral learning methods to complement print methods may be the picture God had in mind to transform people for the kingdom. Let's keep painting.

Chapter 13

Contextualizing Theological Education in Africa: A Case of ECWA Theological Seminary, Jos, Nigeria (JETS)

Bauta D. Motty

In Nigeria, I have attended many book launchings and book dedication services. On some occasions, I have heard the chief launcher or dedicator say, "If you keep money in the bank or a safe, someone may steal it. But if you keep money in a book, no one will steal it." This insinuates that the society or the people do not read books. It also confirms to us that the people, including the local intellectuals, are oral and love to remain so. The question is: *Why are the people not interested in reading?* And what is bad about it? It should be noted that years ago in many church denominations, including mine, reading and writing were required for church membership and position.

The persistent non-reading attitude of the people greatly suggests that orality is a powerful virtue of the society, and trying to abolish it will mean killing the psyche, life, and morality of the people. Orality is the thought and verbal expression in societies where the technologies of literacy (especially writing and print) are unfamiliar to most of the population. The study of orality is closely related to the study of oral tradition.

However, it has broader implications, implicitly touching every aspect of the economics, politics, institutional development, and human development of oral societies. The study of orality has important implications for international development, especially as it relates to the goal of eradicating poverty as well as the process of globalization.

It is worth noting what educational psychologists say about in relation to orality. According to them, we learn by:

- Reading – 10 percent
- Hearing – 20 percent
- Seeing – 30 percent
- Hearing and seeing – 50 percent
- Discussing with others – 75 percent
- Personal experience – 85 percent
- Doing or teaching back – 95 percent

Hence, orality is educative.

I am a minister in a theological context at ECWA Theological Seminary, Jos, Nigeria. For six and a half years I have been in academia, and the difference is clear. I have discovered a number of things in my first semester of teaching:

1. The academic situation is all about literacy, which is after the Western educational system.
2. The instruction is teacher-centered, content-centered, and then student-centered. Thus, a teacher comes to class as "*Mr. Know-it-all.*"
3. Students complete activities designed by the teacher to achieve academic success.
4. The worldview of most students is: "We do not know anything, and so the teacher should give us knowledge."
5. The social structure of Nigeria requires that students are under the teacher in order to "receive knowledge."

6. Most of the students have families with high demands on them.

7. Students work to achieve curricular objectives in order to become critical thinkers.

8. Students respond to positive expectations set by the teacher as they progress through activities.

9. Students are given extrinsic motivators like grades and rewards that motivate them to internalize information and objectively demonstrate their understanding of concepts.

10. The teacher evaluates student work.

My training at Asbury Theological Seminary has helped me greatly. At Asbury, I was exposed to the issues of cultural anthropology, sociology, leadership skills, and the use of arts in Christian ministry. This prepared me for the teaching ministry in Nigeria.

Although I must be committed to my seminary's (JETS) philosophy, vision, mission, and content, I must also adapt to the reality of the students. Therefore, I had to make some modifications in order to make learning an adventure for the students. No matter how educated an African is, he or she is an oral being. Why? Below are a number of reasons.

To be oral is to be relational and people-oriented. Orality is about building relationship. Orality is about interpersonal bonding. An oral person can get along with others and is comfortable with them. Oral people focus on the needs of the people around them in order to accomplish the task; they are concerned with building relationships and keeping people happy so that they can be efficient and productive, and they place more importance on the feelings and happiness of people who will help them achieve the goals set. Relationship is the connection between two or more people in which they are able to share not only their possessions, but also their lives (1 Thess. 2:8).

I have decided to encourage a student-centered teaching method. By this method, students solve problems, answer questions, formulate questions of their own, discuss, explain, debate, and brainstorm during class. They participate in cooperative learning, in which they work in teams on problems and projects under conditions that assure both positive interdependence and individual accountability. We also use inductive teaching and learning, in which students are presented with challenges (questions or problems) and learn the course material in the context of addressing the challenges. This approach includes inquiry-based learning, case-study instruction, problem-based learning, project-based learning, discovery learning, and just-in-time teaching.

Hence, at JETS, each student leads in devotion prior to a class session. No student should attend the class when his or her family member is sick. I wash students' feet during our Leadership course. Each class member should know the names of the other class members and have the ability to visit the residence of a classmate.

To be oral is to be culturally relevant. Culture is central to learning. It plays a role not only in communicating and receiving information, but also in shaping the thinking process of groups and individuals. A pedagogy that acknowledges, responds to, and celebrates fundamental cultures offers full, equitable access to education for students in the Nigerian context.

Culturally-responsive theological teaching is a pedagogy that recognizes the importance of including students' cultural references in all aspects of learning (Ladson-Billings 1994). Some of the characteristics of culturally-responsive teaching in the seminary are: (1) positive perspectives on parents and families, (2) communication of high expectations, (3) learning within the context of culture, (4) student-centered instruction, (5) culturally-mediated instruction, (6) reshaping the curriculum, and (7) teacher as facilitator.

As the National Director and Consultant of Voice For Humanity (VFH) HIV/AIDS program in Kano State in 2005/2006, I rediscovered the necessity of orality in human interaction, especially among the Hausa people at Gaiya and Mai-Makawa.

One of the fringe benefits of orality-based communication methods is relationship building and the development of community. We used culturally-relevant Hausa oral methods of storytelling, folk songs, proverbs, and dramas to disseminate the information to the local people through community, religious leaders, and family heads. The result was tremendous: there was a higher percent increase of the people's HIV awareness, and the people decided to send away all prostitutes in their village, Mai-Makawa. Theological educational method should include the use of local arts.

To be oral is to be transformative. We cannot effect change in others unless we are orally relevant. There is no growth without change and there is no change without touching the heart. Transformative learning is based upon dialogue in an atmosphere of love, trust, and respect. Africans have a very strong sense of "community as educator" (Bray, Clarke, and Stephens 1986, 104) and a high respect for individuals. This high regard for people and relationships augurs well for a positive reception of the types of techniques proposed as fostering critical reflective thought. An attempt to diffuse this educational model should emphasize this participatory aspect of transformative learning.

For example, the Hausa community of Gaiya and Mai-Makawa experienced transformation because the program was within their reach and from their cultural resources. They sent prostitutes away and would not want to see any others in their community. We went to the people through their local leaders. Unless transformation has taken place, we have not succeeded in our communication efforts and strategies.

To be oral is to be dramatic. Orality is also about having a powerful expressive voice—having a powerful singing voice especially suited to the expression of intense emotion, for example, in Nigeria. Drama is often combined with music and dance—the drama in the

ECWA Church today is generally sung throughout; musicals generally include both spoken dialogue and songs.

Today in Nigeria, women are the life of church worship. They dramatize their singing. Their songs are more easily remembered than any song produced from do, re, mi, fa, so, la, ti, do.

To be oral is to be practical. Orality is concerned with matters of fact—actual facts and real-life experience, not theory. It is concerned with what is useful, appropriate, sensible, and likely to be effective. Orality focuses on what is good at solving problems: good at managing matters and dealing with problems and difficulties. For example, someone can be very clever, but not be practical. To be oral is to be plain, functional, and suitable for everyday life.

My participation in the Kaduna State Commission of Inquiry into the cause of social and religious disturbances in the State during the presidential elections in 2011 also helped to shape my oral being. The most important part of the assignment was our personal visits to the affected villages and people. Our appearance on behalf of the government brought relief to some who were ready to commit suicide because their wealth was destroyed. Talking to them was more than memoranda that some wrote to the Commission. Our visits and conversations together brought healing to many. Hence, orality is curative.

To be oral is to be dialogical. The modes of decision making in African culture employ dialogue and consensus. Although this activity is not open to all members of the community (usually only adult males), it nonetheless coincides with the dialogical nature of teaching for critical reflective thought. For example, every ethnic group has a discussion meeting or council. Although the Siyong (the community council of Kaninkon people) is not specifically an educational institution, the fact that dialogue and consensus are the norm, which allows for a chance to bridge from one context to the other. That is why at the beginning of every course session, we talk together as we divide students into groups and they discuss and draw up their expectations or course objectives.

The benefits of this teaching approach strengthens students' motivation, promotes peer communication, builds student-teacher relationships, promotes discovery/active learning, and gives a sense of responsibility for each student's own learning.

To be oral is to be event oriented. The phrase "time management" would not naturally occur in the language of an event-oriented culture. It is a phrase that would only occur to someone coming into such a culture from a time-oriented one. In time-oriented cultures we think of time as a commodity. Our language reflects this when we talk about "spending" or "saving" time and when we talk about "investing" or "wasting" time. The phrase "time is money" would make little sense in an event-oriented culture.

Jesus lived in a culture in which people did not wear watches on their wrists and did not hang clocks on every wall. Sometimes, he responded immediately and went to people; at other times, he delayed his response or withdrew to be alone. In my own course teaching, I make allowance for students to see me without any appointment and am very spontaneous in dealing with my friends, the students.

To be oral is to be traditional and contextual. Oral communities invest considerable energy into basic information management. Storage of information is primarily dependent upon individual or collective recall (Goody 1968, 13-14). Orality is the surrounding conditions—the circumstances or events that form the environment within which communication of a message exists or takes place. As we communicate the message, the words, phrases, or passages that come before and after a particular word or passage in our message, speech, or piece of writing must help to explain its full meaning. And this must be relating to or based upon custom or belief or long-established action or pattern of behavior in a community or group of people that has been handed down from generation to generation. The traditional life of the learners or listeners must be considered.

In my Worldview Course, every student is required to collect at least 50 proverbs of his or her local culture, then find what the Bible says about each proverb and make an application. For example, one proverb says, "The medicine of the sickness of the rich man is in the farm of the poor man." This proverb is about teamwork. In teamwork, every person's presence and contributions are needed. The main issues of this proverb are sickness and medicine and rich man and poor man. What does the Bible say about teamwork?

In my Homiletics Course, I encourage students to use stories to introduce their sermons. They use a lot of African arts for their ethnodoxology. Art is any heightened form of communication; it may have aspects of song, dance, storytelling, proverb, visual arts, drama, and architectural arts. Ethnodoxology is about calling all peoples to worship in their heart language. A former student sent me a text saying, "Using local arts, storytelling, local metaphors, and dramas has revolutionized our worship services."

To be oral is to be participatory. Oral learners mostly rely upon and trust in the technique for learning that is in a "close, empathetic, and communal association" with others whom they know. In traditional African education, participant observation was, and remains, one of the main methods of education (Bray, Clarke, and Stephens 1986, 106). This is a form of experiential learning. In this traditional system, learning is active. Learners are not passive, but should actively engage in the learning process. This also is a point of similarity with transformative learning. Although the form of this participation may vary from traditional education, the fact that it is experience-based provides a point of continuity.

Hence, in most of the course sessions, I invite an outsider and specialist to address the class, and the students take notes and either share their understanding or submit their notes for marking. The invited guest teacher, class members, and teacher form a community of learners. Students participate in developing the class course objectives.

To be oral is to be situational rather than abstract. In African cultures, concepts are used in a way that minimizes abstraction, focusing to the greatest extent possible on objects and situations directly known by the speaker (Luria 1931, 1-2). Oral learners always use real objects with which they are familiar. Hence, my foot-washing session helps students understand what Jesus did. This act always creates a sense of remorse in students who weep when I am washing their feet. The biblical Trinitarian doctrine can be made simple by the use of the African Trinitarian concept. We should use visual aids to teach in Africa.

Conclusion

Theological education in Africa is in dire need of culturally-relevant curriculum and sensitive ethnomethodology in training local pastors and teachers. The theological education curricula must be theocentric and anthropocentric. The Bible and the African culture and worldview should help in the formulation of teaching materials in our theological institutions. Christianity without indigenous discipleship is Christianity without Christ, and Christianity without Christ is mere religion, and a religion will surely disappear with time (Acts 5:34-39). Christianity without indigenous discipleship is a denial of the pre-gospel existence of God in the context.

Our theological teaching methods should require: (1) putting subject-teaching objectives together with student-learning objectives; (2) that we use interactions mostly at the beginning and the end of each course session/facilitation; (3) class sessions not be confined to the four-walled classroom alone; (4) that in leadership, we are models like Jesus; (5) the teaching atmosphere to be interactive and participatory, so that students are helped to identify with what they are learning; (6) students' families to be given priority over class attendance, and class attendance to be given priority over written coursework; and (7) that every class member must know the names of other course mates.

Questions:
1. What skills do the pastors and teachers need in order to develop a curriculum relevant to the context for theological training today in Africa?
2. Why are our theological institutions hesitant to make theological training culturally sensitive?

Chapter 14

Theological Education as Incarnational Missiology: Empowering and Affirming Oral Learners in Oral Culture Pastor Training

Mark M. Overstreet

In eager anticipation of the dialogue during this consultation, this paper will address the nature of empowering and affirming oral learners in the context of theological education. This task will be accomplished by assessing the model of pastor training and leader development among oral cultures I currently implement around the world in non-formal, Fourth World contexts (which includes informational capital, poverty, and social exclusion).

Additionally, I will address the contributions of external assessment instruments for oral culture programs, discovering areas to learn and (re)discover in all sectors of theological education for oral learners. Finally, I will create a list of questions that may guide the discussion as the consultation seeks to discover best practices for oral learner empowerment and affirmation in pastoral training. In all of these tasks, I will address the challenges of working with oral cultures, moving the dialogue forward for the concrete benefit of oral learners and any potential role one may serve in the future of theological education among oral cultures.

In order to understand properly the nature of empowering and affirming oral learners, it is important to discuss a few matters as introduction. First, I resist a binary understanding of literacy and orality. Binary discussions of these communication preferences can be unfortunate and counterproductive. Researchers are beginning to understand the complexity of the interface between orality and literacy, especially in advancing world contexts.

While the benefits of literacy should not be neglected, time and space constrain our focus here to the task of training oral cultures. Modern theological education has presented apparent myopia in neglecting the potential for theological learning among oral communities. Furthermore, within the arc of theological studies, there exists today an anachronistic print bias in much of the modern literature in biblical and theological scholarship. In Christian missiology, however, the growth of the disciplines of linguistics, cultural anthropology, sociolinguistics, and ethnographics reveals a rich collection of accessible media for oral learners in the ancient world.

Second, I am a hermeneutical realist. Communication is not neutral. Translation is not neutral. Hermeneutics is not neutral. Theology is not neutral. One's worldview shapes every aspect of human understanding. Each individual interprets meaning in light of the "horizons of expectation" that have been shaped by the communities to which the individual belongs (Thiselton, 2009, 65). Thus, the interests of the interpretive community shape all interpretation. Religion, family life, education, traditions, economics, and social structures all inform interpretive ethos. Just as cultures and languages may shape the translation of the word of God, Bible translations can contour the way a people within a culture live out the faith. Ministers, missionaries, and theological educators are no exception. Equally, oral learners are shaped by oral culture in every aspect of their existence.

The following considerations flow from observations and experiences from evaluated programs in theological education, evangelism and discipleship, and humanitarian programs in oral learning environments.

Empower and affirm oral learners through pastoral training. Through oral culture programs, I serve communities through local partnerships that provide indigenous pastors and leaders an orality-based platform for existing church leadership development, discipleship, outreach, evangelism, and planting new churches. In every program, mission partners share with the local partners a common vision for incarnational, orality-based pastors who are biblically sound and are planting/pastoring oral-culture churches engaged in whole person ministry. As a result of listening to the local community, facilitated conversations with numerous leaders within each oral community generate a program shaped by local socio-political, socio-economic, cultural, and linguistic preferences.

As missiologists and anthropologists grow to understand the complexity of media preferences among oral learners, the contour of oral culture programs should conform more effectively to serve oral communities in ministry. Shaped by an evangelical understanding of God's accommodation in revelation, it is my hope that theological educators strive to build programs that support local language and local leadership infrastructure for effectiveness and sustainability.

Pastoral training programs for oral cultures serve local communities with a leadership development program that empowers and affirms each oral learner through incarnational missiology, which cultivates leaders who see the transformation of their communities and cultures by the gospel.

Affirm oral cultures through Christological service. Theological education serves the Church. As a manifestation of the Body of Christ, theological education should reveal God's character and attributes. As God, Jesus lived as a man among humanity (incarnation). The Logos revealed himself to the cosmos through the person of a local man. He embraced local culture, spoke the local language, and lived with his audience in mind. Theological education is incarnational.

Just as Jesus revealed himself in human flesh, theological education for the Church should dwell among the locals, proclaiming truth through local culture, custom, language, and principle. Theological education should be contextual. The Logos revealed himself in a specific linguistic and cultural context, as a first-century Jewish man in Roman Palestine. Theological education best serves the Church when it includes incarnate and contextual proclamation.

Empower oral cultures through concrete inputs. From years of evaluation feedback and local leader grassroots input, the basis for local partnerships among oral learners is based upon a mutual mission and vision to provide theological education that models a ministry rooted in an experiential, participatory, dynamic, small group ministry. The learning environment embraces a searcher model, an incremental discovery process that relies upon feedback from implementation. From these conversations, concrete modeling, community-driven, and holistic approaches to theological education trickle up from emerging leaders.

Empower oral cultures through healthy partnership. Empowerment begins before theological education. Some acknowledge a complex tension between host community and mission agency. As a result, stronger partnerships are built upon principled agreement of local mission, values, goals, accountability, and measurable outcomes. Additionally, partnerships in mission should be characterized by a foundation of respect, trust, and dignity rooted in the image of God. All partners communicate openly concerning the principles and processes with the input and agreement of all partners, especially for local decision making and conflict resolution.

Through growth-oriented, open communication channels, all partner relationships serve to accomplish specific locally-grown purposes and may take on new local goals over time. Partners prioritize clear outputs and outcomes through active listening, acknowledging one another's needs and self-interests, working to develop a common language of success. Partners seek a common understanding of the balance of power among parties, which enables resources (e.g., fiscal, physical, spiritual) to be shared and communicated openly.

Partners invite regular feedback from all participants in the partnership, seeking the common goal of continuously improving measurable results. All expectations, goals, outputs, and outcomes are spoken, shared, and recorded for all partners. This trust builds upon identified strengths and assets, and also works to address needs and increase capacity for all partners. In this relationship, each member shares all benefits and all accomplishments. The partnership dialogue affirms the dignity of both parties, and the process builds relationship for common ministry, enabling local, grassroots comprehension and action from the indigenous partner.

Affirm oral cultures through healthy prerequisites. In order to begin a pastoral training program where all partner communities are primarily oral in culture, the indigenous leaders recognize that fact and understand the need for an orality-based approach to training. All partners listen to the indigenous partner, as they desire to reach beyond communities that have some existing presence of the church and some existing need for church leaders. Also, evidence of a Christ-ward movement is present, hence the need for new depth through oral pastor training and church planting. Finally, there exists a small team of indigenous leaders already working in the communities through whom to implement the program. This team of indigenous leaders has a vision for evangelism and church planting.

Empower oral cultures through local implementation. In order for pastoral training to be implemented successfully in oral cultures, the following orality concepts maximize oral culture empowerment when incorporated into the program strategy.

First, *the education is locally spoken (heart language), locally led, experiential, contextual, and concrete, not abstract or academic.* Training discussions take place in mother tongue, local dialects, avoiding national, trade, and academic languages. Accelerating local leader presence may be accomplished by reducing outsider presence in training and program execution. I call this "reducing the white man's footprint," and of course, the color of one's foot is not my primary concern. Sustainability and dependency remain priority interests in the mission world. Could a program be more effective if local leaders who speak local dialects take the lead earlier and more fully in all phases?

Second, *all learning is group learning, not individualistic, affirming the nature of our oral culture partners.* Dialogue-driven methods empower local leaders to model and reproduce this learning environment to their disciples. Third, *the training is implemented through andragogical discussion, not pedagogical methods.* Discipleship is circular and redundant, not linear and hierarchical. Fourth, *all content is driven by local, contextual, applied learning, not external abstract knowledge.*

Affirm oral cultures through local holistic content. As a result, local partners build content that sprouts from their culture, yielding content consistent with their community. With the indigenous content bias, the program yields worldview-sensitive content derived from the word of God in the local community. Together with the word, all partners identify local community development needs. The community needs are great, and local leaders want to accelerate access to holistic solutions to physical challenges in the village (e.g., clean water, sanitation, health, hygiene, HIV/AIDS, democracy, malaria, corruption, character building, peace building, tuberculosis, leprosy, suicide). From this discussion, the team works with content experts to build holistic support for whole-person ministry. All of this content is built in community, by community, and discussed through informed facilitated listening groups.

Empower oral cultures through local distribution. The Oral Culture Pastor Training Program begins as a three-cycle (approximately

3.5 years) program that develops and trains a minimum of 220 oral leaders. From that genesis, we plan for the program to facilitate daily evangelism, weekly discipleship, and new church plants over the 3.5-year timeframe. Each of the three phases completes a cycle of training, with the second and third cycle being wider and deeper. Each cycle has a number of main components.

1. The local team spends several weeks grappling with worldview, contextualization and orality issues as they relate to the targeted communities.

2. The local team spends several weeks identifying Bible stories, current life dramas, songs, and indigenous proverbs/stories to address community issues and introduce God's Word. They also give directions for living life as followers of Jesus through the word.

3. The local team spends weeks composing, recording, and editing audio content for use on Mobile Schools (audio playback devices). A minimum of 30 Bible stories will be recorded, as well as a minimum of ten current life dramas focused on identified community issues.

4. The local leaders spend 30 weeks of small listening/discussion groups for participating leaders in training. Based upon local leader feedback, the pace generally averages one Bible segment per week. The groups meet at least once a week and the leaders concurrently reach out to friends, family, and other members of their villages and communities with the biblical and humanitarian content. This component serves the community through basic evangelism and discipleship and life skills.

5. The local team spends several weeks assessing the impact through third-party evaluation and identifying leaders to proceed to the next cycle of training.

The teams discuss the content for themselves and how to present this worldview-sensitive, contextualized gospel to an oral culture audience. The Bible stories linked to current community issues, needs, or challenges enable the oral culture community to hear and receive the stories, while they also grow and guard against misapplication of biblical content.

As syncretism (Christo-paganism) is commonplace in oral cultures where orality issues as well as contextualization issues are not considered, this remains another function of the oral program that the indigenous partners seek to understand and put into practice. These concepts are not often grasped and practiced on the basis of a single five-day training session. To that end, the entire training structure is built to give the indigenous leaders and pastors an apprenticeship in doing complete orality-based ministry.

The second and third cycles are designed to take the lessons learned by the pastors, as well as the third-party evaluation and think specifically about these three disciplines as they relate to the teaching/ preaching of God's word. As a result, the pastors are the beneficiaries of a three-way conversation between the word of God, the receptor culture, and the maturation of the indigenous church. By the time the program reaches its final phase, the pastors can apply the word of God to their culture with great skill and faithfulness from multiple years of cycles saturated in the word of God.

Empower oral cultures through third-party evaluation. Informed by biblical stewardship, field partners seek the wise use of resources that have been invested by funding partners for pastoral training programs. Up to 15 percent of each program budget is earmarked for third-party evaluation. Consistent with kingdom values, this discipline provides outside assessment and review for each of our oral learner programs. Some foundations and discerning donors are asking new questions during the funding and planning phases that precede each project. *What are the measurable results? What are the outputs? What is the timeframe for achieving these landmarks? How will one know when the partnership has arrived at its destination?*

Third-party evaluations serve the partnership, providing objective empirical data confirming the progress and noting discernible challenges in every program. Statistics are gathered through pre-content and post-content oral learner surveys to determine impact in three domains: knowledge, attitude, and behavior. Every program seeks life-changing transformation. Third-party evaluations provide the data the partners seek to confirm areas of progress and correct areas where more attention may be needed. Each written third-party evaluation measures a program's impact in areas of ministry and humanitarian content.

Requiring third-party evaluation means someone from the outside analyzes each project executed. Before continuing the next phases of partnership, the third-party evaluator conducts interviews with the oral learners and the communities in which they work and minister. Like no other tool, the third-party evaluation consistently serves as one of the most effective learning tools for ministry and work among oral cultures.

Third-party evaluation helps us improve ministry to oral learners. Like an external audit, third-party evaluation lends objectivity to partnership and its development. In this way, the partners implement the same kind of transparency and accountability with donors that were cultivated with indigenous cohorts. Third-party evaluations provide structure to program execution, offering recommended course corrections for ongoing program improvement.

Affirm oral cultures through local feedback. Through local partner dialogue, all partners reengage each visit with question-based feedback. Oral culture partners improve every process of our partnerships through their insights. In the spirit of local feedback and for our purposes in this consultation, I would like to offer some questions for your consideration:

1. How would one build experimental freedom into oral culture programs?
2. How would one promote greater learner autonomy through

learner independence in an oral culture?

3. In what way would one build active reflective forms of learner engagement and provide creative support to warrant a holistic learning environment?

4. In what ways could a partner provide purposeful and imaginative engagement in the following areas: decision making, reflection, learner empowerment?

5. How could one measure learner fulfillment and enjoyment in oral culture programs?

6. Could one confine group engagement with oral learners to typical teacher-pupil relations in participatory, inclusive model of oral culture ministry?

7. How could one create imaginative engagement within oral cultures, by allowing them to create the genre new media?

8. How does one measure and ensure the accuracy of oral culture content within a particular oral context?

9. How does a partnership ensure collective responsibility for a program and shared achievement in the outputs?

10. Who defines the terms of authentic instructional contexts?

11. How do all partners model commitment to a program? How do they model trust in the process, test the process, review the process, recommit to the process?

12. How does one measure motivation and enthusiasm among oral learners?

13. Who defines ownership in a program?

14. In leadership development, what methods of formative feedback result in optimal local leader life change?

15. In what ways does instructor ethos communicate empowerment and affirmation?

16. In oral cultures where knowledge and accountability is communal, how is personal achievement and individual responsibility measured for growth?

17. With transformation as a goal, what role could assessment and third-party evaluation have in modeling the practices the partners are seeking to have the pastors implement in their ministry?

18. What input should local partners have at the strategic and tactical level to be consistent with outcome-based approaches they are responsible for executing?

19. How would one measure the varying role gestures, postures, expressions, tone, and mood play among oral cultures, especially given the cultural context of communication?

20. In the absence of a reliable translation in the mother tongue, what level of expertise is acceptable for transitioning from available written translation into the language group's mother tongue and oral tradition?

21. How could one build a system of accuracy in translation from a written, literate copy of scripture to an oral culture context where written language barriers exist?

22. What constitutes an acceptable level of measurable accuracy for an oral culture?

23. How might one best measure understanding among listeners who have access to audio reading of a scripture translation?

24. What constitutes an unacceptable burden for accountability and accuracy among oral cultures?

25. In what ways are you currently evaluating the following program data: questionnaires, field notes, reflective comments, interviews?

26. What constitutes success of an oral learner program?

Through the power of God's gospel, may we pursue together with each partner a shared common mission, stronger relationships, built-in mutuality, fluidity/openness to change goals over time, clear and open communication, balance of power through humility, proper feedback loops, improvement mechanisms, identification of strengths, commitment to build strengths, and shared accomplishments/shared benefits for all involved. May all of our service in theological education be conformed to his image, the Chief Servant, Shepherd, King, for the fame of his Name to every tribe, tongue, and nation, until he appears.

Chapter 15

Responding to the Articles in Perspective IV

M. David Sills

A Response to Teaching Oral Learners in Institutional Settings

Overview

W. Jay Moon offers characteristics of oral learners through three distinct examples. These examples illustrate the ways in which the characteristics of orality are manifest distinctly in different contexts. It is Moon's contention that the educator should determine whether those being taught are oral learners and then incorporate the noted characteristics, allowing them to inform the educational style employed.

Distinct Contribution

Moon's paper offers three distinct contributions. First, his illustrations of the three distinct examples through which he reflects on oral learning are helpful for contradicting the perception that oral cultures are uneducated and unintelligent.

Second, in addition to the characteristics of oral learners that Moon recounts, the contribution he offers in the form of the "Oral vs.

Print Learning Preferences" table is a helpful overview that could be used to communicate a broad understanding of orality to those who have had limited exposure.

Third, while suggestions for teaching oral learners are not particularly unique, Moon's approach to frame these suggestions from the perspective of the oral learner is helpful. He illustrates inadequacies of prevailing Western models of education for oral learners. He also provides a contouring perspective by communicating the implications of the culture from the perspective of one within it.

Point of Critique

Syncretism: While Moon's three examples are helpful for identifying commonalities in oral learners across distinct cultures, the illustration of the Native American raises concerns of syncretism. This illustration inadvertently illustrates the ease with which contextualization that is not critical contextualization can slip into syncretism. It could be open to accusations of a wholesale acceptance of the characteristics of oral learners as the standard to which instruction must conform. However, a model of critical contextualization should always be employed to ensure that the Bible is informing culture rather than culture superseding biblical teachings.

Issues for Further Consideration

Moon wisely points out the significance of mnemonics as it relates to oral instruction, which is one of the most powerful advantages of oral learners over high literates. As such, the potential implications of mnemonics as it relates to biblical instruction should be explored and developed. Another point of consideration might be whether the model of encouraging memorization of actual biblical text should be more normative in discipleship, leadership training, and theological education, while Chronological Bible Storying could be primarily used in evangelism.

Questions for Further Consideration

1. Is the "Oral vs. Print Learning Preferences" table complete as listed? Are there adjustments to be made? How might this resource be used?
2. How can we best train oral learners to recognize and avoid syncretism?
3. How can we utilize mnemonics for biblical instruction as a component of discipleship and theological education?
4. How can discipleship and theological education be accomplished within languages that do not yet have a translated biblical text?

A Response to Contextualizing Theological Education in Africa: A Case of ECWA Theological Seminary, Jos, Nigeria (JETS)

Overview

Bauta Motty offers a helpful overview of key characteristics of African oral cultures. These characteristics are most clearly articulated to represent those within church leadership and theological education. However, they also provide a framework for a broader understanding of oral cultures. Motty clearly demonstrates that oral cultures are relational rather than data oriented and thus necessitate a distinct approach to education and instructional materials. He concludes with a strong call to develop teaching materials that are contextualized for oral cultures, with a consideration to how they learn and what they value.

Distinct Contribution

Motty writes from the perspective of one actively engaged in the work of educating leaders in a culture that cultivates and values orality. This emic perspective is extremely helpful to push us past our Western tendencies of linear logic and the traditional trappings of a highly-literate education as necessary components of training programs.

Motty also offers a unique contribution through his emphasis on servant leadership in the role of the teacher. He reflects that oral cultures are not opposed to strong leadership and actually tend to regard teachers very highly. He meets the challenge to embrace cultural preferences while avoiding any danger of paternalism through servant leadership. He speaks of washing his students' feet as an exercise in class, illustrating two key distinctions between Western education models and models in oral cultures. First, the emphasis on relationship in a shared community is the strongest bond in the oral culture whereas achievement and results are typically the primary goals in Western models of education. Second, Motty demonstrates the participatory nature of oral cultures. Western models of education typically focus on data; Motty's contribution illustrates clearly the preeminence given to learning that occurs in mentoring relationships.

Points of Critique

Critical contextualization: Motty does an excellent job of educating the reader on the characteristics of an oral culture. This information is undoubtedly helpful for contextualizing a message to a target audience that consists of oral learners. However, he does not address any characteristics that should be informed and changed by biblical teaching, which could give the impression that he believes that all aspects of orality should be automatically embraced and incorporated in the education model. As with any culture, the characteristics of an oral culture should be processed through the lens of critical contextualization prior to developing the contextualized ministry.

Issues for Further Consideration

First, Motty's examination of the characteristics of the African oral context is a helpful beginning to develop a broader viewpoint on the characteristics of oral contexts across distinct people groups. Developing such a framework, building from Motty's contribution as well as other papers presented, will be helpful for developing practical training paradigms.

Second, each of the characteristics identified either as part of the African oral context or a broader oral tradition should be evaluated in light of biblical teaching on that topic. Any characteristic or tendency that is contrary to the biblical model of life and godliness should be approached from the standpoint of bringing it into conformity with the word of God rather than as a matter to inform a contextualized training model.

Third, Motty's overarching conclusion that there is need for a culturally-relevant curriculum should be regarded as of overwhelming importance for all those working to reach and teach oral cultures. The resources that do exist for intercultural pastoral training are both primarily literate as well as wholly Western in approach. Until this is made a priority for concentrated research, it is unlikely to come to fruition, yet it remains an overwhelming need in the cause of Christ in oral cultures.

Questions for Further Consideration

1. What skills are necessary to develop a culturally-appropriate curriculum model for oral cultures?
2. What can be done to encourage theological institutions to make training culturally sensitive?
3. What characteristics of those listed by Motty as normative for African oral contexts are normative across all oral cultures?
4. What model might be effective for teaching biblical content that cannot be storied in oral cultures?

A Response to Theological Education as Incarnational Missiology: Empowering and Affirming Oral Learners in Oral Culture Pastor Training

Overview

Mark Overstreet offers an evaluation of the various issues central to developing a holistic, incarnational model of theological education within an oral culture. Overstreet rejects a binary understanding of literacy and orality, which is fairly representative in the field, and emphasizes a holistic view of theological education. He reflects a healthy view of indigenous leadership and a realistic recognition of the role of contextualization. He concludes the paper with 26 questions to be considered at the consultation.

Distinct Contribution

Overstreet offers two distinct contributions to the discussion of theological education among oral cultures. First, he emphasizes holistic ministry as an intentional component of theological education. The way in which the incarnational model could identify and manifest a holistic expression in each culture represents an area of education and ministry development that is sometimes ignored. Given the growing awareness of physical and social needs as a component of global ministry, this is a helpful contribution to the discussion.

Overstreet offers a second distinct point for consideration by raising the issue of third-party evaluation. This element not only introduces a third party into the relationship and program, it also necessitates a highly scientific evaluation process. Overstreet advocates allocating up to 15 percent of the program funding for this process, which he explains is to be done at the conclusion of each project and executed prior to continuing the next phase of the partnership. With a comparison to an external audit, he contends that this will lend itself to objectivity and partnership development.

Points of Critique

Third-party evaluation: I appreciate the desire to be strategic and to have objective feedback on programs as they are being developed. However, while Overstreet does an excellent job of articulating cultural distinctions that must be incorporated and establishes a framework that is distinctly incarnational, the model of evaluation offered is distinctly Western and scientific.

This model would be an excellent tool of evaluation in a Western context where information is presented (and therefore gathered) in a scientific model and in which systems are static and linear for such systemic comparison. However, I have very rarely seen such a system in theological education outside of the United States. It tends to be only within the literate cultures that this model could be effectively used and appreciated as an evaluation tool. The need for evaluation is certainly accurate, but a scientific, data-centric model would likely be ineffective in an oral culture. Moreover, as a reproducible model of education, it would model to nationals the importance of such third-party evaluations and hinder 2 Timothy 2:2 in places where this is not feasible.

Issues for Further Consideration

Although Chronological Bible Storying is an incredibly effective model of evangelism in oral cultures, theological education and pastoral preparation have proven far more difficult with this model in the absence of a static text. Point-in-time teaching can utilize stories for specific teaching, but other narrative forms of teaching are required. Oral methodologies in pastoral training and theological education must go beyond initial evangelism and discipleship when working with oral cultures.

Given the complexities of oral worldviews and the tendency toward syncretism, it is essential to train up leaders in the full counsel of the word of God. The nature of much of the biblical text that is most applicable to matters of ecclesiology, such as is found in the Epistles, is difficult to story. Thus, there is a need to develop a more comprehensive cycle of theological education that employs other forms of narrative instruction within the incarnational model presented by Overstreet.

A second area for further consideration is the criteria for the third-party evaluator and the form of the evaluation. If a third-party evaluator is used, consideration must be given to whether or not the evaluator will have the necessary prerequisite knowledge of oral cultures, the specific culture being evaluated, and ministry challenges unique to each community. Principles should also be developed for relationships to the missionary or indigenous leaders so that objectivity and transparency are cultivated from the start.

In addition to the criteria of the evaluator, the form of evaluation should be developed further. As previously noted, the scientific, data-centric approach proposed does not adequately incorporate the realities of working within oral cultures. Overstreet's call for objective evaluation is very helpful, but the specifics on who should do that and how it should be done, and who pays for it need further development.

Questions for Further Consideration

1. How does one measure and ensure the accuracy of oral-culture content within a particular oral context?

2. In oral cultures where knowledge and accountability is communal, how is personal achievement and individual responsibility measured for growth?

3. With transformation as a goal, what role could assessment and third-party evaluation have in modeling the practices the partners desire for pastors to implement in their ministry?

4. In the absence of a reliable translation in the mother tongue, what level of expertise is acceptable for transitioning from available written translation into the language group's mother tongue and oral tradition?

5. If the training must be done in the tribal dialect or heart language of a culture rather than utilizing the trade language or dominant culture language such as Swahili, Spanish, or English, who would the teachers be in the thousands of cultures that lack translations and missionaries? And how can the teaching occur in languages that lack terms for biblical and theological concepts?

6. How can one build a system of accuracy in translation from a written, literate copy of scripture to an oral culture context where written language barriers exist?

7. What must be taught for a pastor in an oral culture to be considered trained?

8. What constitutes success of an oral learner program?

EPILOGUE

Grant Lovejoy

Beyond Literate Western Models

Six months have passed since the consultation where these chapters were discussed. They generated lively and enthusiastic discussion among the participants. One participant told me that after this consultation he would never think about theological education the same way. If the past six months are any indication, it will have a substantial impact on others, too. Consider some of the activities that have taken place or are planned as a result of the consultation.

Current and Future Discussions

Participants developed new relationships with others interested in the same topics. This has led to further discussions, stimulated new ideas for research, and encouraged those who wondered if anyone else shared their passion for equipping oral learners. Some theological institutions have had a full faculty report and a discussion about the consultation. A similar mini-global consultation is planned in Asia for June 2013 to discuss these topics.

Planning has begun for a series of regional Orality Forum events to be held on seminary campuses in the United States beginning in 2014. Each forum will focus on orality and theological education. Forum planners hope to stimulate discussion of these issues within each host institution and among other attendees from the region.

Additionally, a group of theological educators heard about the Wheaton consultation and chose orality as a plenary topic at the triennial meeting of the Asia Theological Association scheduled for August 2013. Reports from the consultation have also encouraged missionary strategists who are considering how best to contextualize theological education for oral environments.

Publication

Evangelical Missions Quarterly is in dialogue with several consultation participants about publishing articles on aspects of orality. The International Orality Network (ION) has launched the *Orality Journal*, an electronic publication designed to give a platform to discuss the impact orality can have on church life and theological education. It will publish articles by consultation participants in several future issues.

ION has also released an annotated bibliography on orality that will be updated periodically so that people interested in this topic can more easily identify pertinent sources. (The bibliography and the *Orality Journal* are available free of charge from the ION website: orality.net)

Coincidentally, a 2013 video, "Man of Peace: The Storytellers of Odisha," tells how a shift from ineffective literate strategies to oral approaches has transformed thousands of lives in Odisha (Orissa), India. In a state notorious for beating Christian pastors, burning church buildings, and destroying Christians' homes, the gospel has spread rapidly and brought peace. The local people no longer fear Christianity as a foreign religion that will destroy their culture.

Through church planters' use of storytelling, indigenous music, drama, dance, and other communication forms to communicate the Bible, the people of Odisha have come to understand that they can be thoroughly biblical in their beliefs and practices and still retain their cultural identity. They now use their treasured art forms to worship the God of the Bible instead of the gods and goddesses they previously worshiped.

Implementation

In sub-Saharan Africa, the Africa Theological Seminary and Jos [Nigeria] Evangelical Theological Seminary are both experimenting with orality within their curricula and in their classrooms. ATS is implementing these innovations on multiple campuses. The Oral Bible Storytelling Training affiliated with the New India Bible Seminary continues to use oral methods in its program.

Other oral training processes described at the consultation continue to grow in their reach and impact. Hearing what our practitioners are doing gave many of us fresh ideas. I was not the only one who was moved by Bauta Motty's description of the intensely pastoral (my term) identity that he has embraced in his seminary classroom in Jos. As he described the highly relational approach that he considers absolutely essential for effective theological education in oral contexts, I thought about faculty members who leave the classroom quickly, make a beeline for their office, and often close the door on students in order to devote their energies to research and writing. What a contrast in perspectives and practices!

Motty's description of his approach also reminded me of a conversation I had with the academic dean of a prominent Bible college in the U.S. The dean told me that he had tried to recruit faculty members who would meet students for coffee or meals, invite students into their homes, pray with them regularly, and do ministry together. That's what their students said they wanted from faculty members.

But the dean said that finding faculty members who wanted that role was surprisingly difficult. This, apparently, was not how young PhD graduates wanted to spend their time. The dean said that he wanted to foster interaction between his faculty and students outside the classroom so much so that he offered to pay for faculty members' lunch twice a week if they would eat it with a handful of students in the campus dining room. Even then, few faculty members took him up on it. The only exceptions to this were the faculty members who had previously been missionaries. They entered eagerly into discipling or mentoring relationships with students. Once he discovered this pattern, the dean increasingly turned to the mission community when he searched for new faculty members.

This example reminds us that theological education involves the interplay of many factors, not least of which are the divergent understandings that faculty members, administrators, students, board members, and constituents have about what is supposed to happen in theological education. Some theological institutions assert that the discipling and spiritual formation of students is the responsibility of the churches. That viewpoint, however, seems to be on the decline partly because of the influence of the churches of the Global South and East, who take a much more holistic view of these things.

The *Cape Town Commitment* of 2010, ratified by 5,000 evangelical leaders drawn primarily from the Global South and East, says, "We strongly encourage seminaries, and all those who deliver leadership training programmes, to focus more on spiritual and character formation, not only on imparting knowledge or grading performance, and we heartily rejoice in those that already do so as part of comprehensive 'whole person' leadership development."

Theological schools in the West may also make this shift. They know that many students in their classes have not been discipled adequately; students need intentional discipling and mentoring. Motty's chapter states powerfully what anyone who studies orality discovers:

oral cultures are intensely relational, face to face, and interactive in their communication. They have a strong sense of community and are generally less individualistic. They do not separate truth from life or theory from practice as readily as other cultures may. Any effort to train or educate people from oral cultures must address this reality. Doing so may alter the very identity of the training programs, their leaders, and those who teach. Tectonic shifts may eventually be necessary.

Fortunately, we can begin with smaller, less wrenching changes. Individual teachers and programs can begin making changes long before any institution-wide shifts take place. Existing seminaries and training programs can initiate smaller adjustments to make their programs more accessible and beneficial to oral learners without making substantial changes in the curriculum.

Much of the innovation in theological education for oral learners takes place in informal learning endeavors and non-formal learning programs. These settings provide opportunities for innovation. David Irving, Jackson Day, Jeff Singerman, and LaNette Thompson described the various innovative informal and non-formal training approaches with which they are or have been involved. Quizzing them about the innovations they have made stimulated our participants to think of new possibilities.

Miriam Adeney's response to David Irving and Jackson Atkins not only highlighted important features of what they are doing and raised significant questions, but Adeney challenged us to keep our training efforts balanced:

- "Good methods are not enough: what we teach about God"
- "Good theology is not enough: what we learn about culture"
- "Good content is not enough: methods matter"

Her emphasis on keeping these three components in any training and to integrate them was a welcome reminder. Throughout the consultation, participants frequently reminded one another that we are dealing with a multi-dimensional reality and must avoid the mistake of acting as if methods alone, or content alone, or any other single factor alone, is the key.

This emphasis on considering all of these elements in their relationship to each other was reflected also in the structure of the meeting. The steering committee (of which I was a part) chose to introduce all four perspectives on the first day so that our participants could consider them simultaneously in their interrelatedness rather than discussing them in isolation from one another.

This freedom to experiment and innovate is a golden opportunity, but to make the most of it, those who run such programs need to be careful to do good planning, implementation, and follow up that includes student assessment and program evaluation. One important contribution informal and non-formal programs could make to the larger theological training and education realm is to document carefully and consistently over periods of time how their training methods have achieved the learning outcomes. This paper trail is essential for establishing credibility with many institutions, financial supporters, and accrediting organizations, who want reassurance that these oral approaches do deliver what they claim to deliver.

Schools can also innovate in smaller ways. They can provide workshops to teach faculty members how to recognize the intersections of their discipline with oral forms of learning and communication. They can explain how to incorporate more oral art forms in their teaching approaches, and how to utilize learning activities that are better suited toward students with high oral preference. They can also explain why it is important whenever possible to include learning outcomes that require oral performance, and how to develop forms of assessment that enable oral students to demonstrate their learning. Phil Walker, Irving, Moon, and Motty provided a number of suggestions along these lines.

Existing theological seminaries, because they already have established patterns, may find it difficult to make wholesale changes quickly. Nevertheless, because they have faculty, students, curriculum, and facilities, they also have the opportunity to make dramatic changes. Already several institutions are moving in this direction and seem poised to pave the way for others who will follow after them.

Presentations by Phil Walker (Chancellor) and Emmanuel Chemengich (Principal) were especially helpful in this regard because their multi-campus Africa Theological Seminary is further down this path of systemic institutional change to orality. There was knowing laughter from our participants (many of whom serve in academic positions) as Walker and Chemengich admitted that *not everyone* in their faculty is enthusiastic about the changes they are implementing.

Mary Verghese, in contrast, described the Oral Bible Storytelling Training, which had orality as a key component from its inception. This program is affiliated with a sympathetic institution run by the same ministry that runs the Oral Bible Storytelling Training. The founders of the new program, with its extensive oral element, did not ask the seminary to make major changes to its own programs. This strategy of establishing a parallel training associated with an existing institution may be a more feasible option in some settings. The two training programs actually intersect in certain respects—this was by design. One motive for it is the hope that the seminary will see the benefits of doing training in a more oral fashion. Verghese said that it is too soon to determine how much influence this linkage will have on the seminary.

In fact, new training programs like this may be the best opportunity to implement what the consultation called the "andragogical perspective." However, it should be applied to existing programs as well. Having initially suggested the technical term "andragogical" to the steering team, I think in retrospect it would have been better not to use it.

As Thompson pointed out briefly, the term has taken on some intellectual baggage that we would be wise to avoid. The steering team's concern (and mine) was to raise the issues related to the fact that the vast majority of oral training is done with adult learners. One of the advantages of orally-based training is that it can include a wider range of adults, including those who never went to school or whose educational skills have faded with time. It is not unusual to have middle-aged or older men and women in our training. Some of these are community leaders. Surely, we recognize the foolishness of treating them as if they were children. Yet at times existing educational models reinforce an unhealthy adult-child pattern of relationship.

Some cultures perpetuate a teacher-pupil relationship that is a world apart from Jesus' example. In these settings the teacher is the unquestioned master of the classroom and authority on all subjects, the shaming of students is a frequent form of "motivation," and students are expected to learn and repeat what they are taught rather than think for themselves or innovate. These practices are bad enough with children; they are even worse in educating adults.

In educating adults, we need to recognize that they have their own goals for their learning, which are often very practical and task-specific. They desire to shape their learning to meet these goals. If we do not meet those needs, they may soon stop attending. Adult learners have abundant life experience; consequently, they have a lot to contribute to most discussions and expect to contribute it, especially if they are successful in their vocation, heads of families, community leaders, and so forth.

Mature adults usually expect to determine how the subject matter applies to their lives. They will make these decisions themselves; it is not for teachers to arrogate to themselves the right to tell adult learners what to do. In any effort to include more oral elements in our training and educational programs, we need to give full consideration of treating adult learners as adults. We involve them in determining the desired outcome of the training and the means by which we will work together to help them achieve it. We deliberately and consistently interact with them instead of lecturing to them hour after hour. We respect their input and treat them as responsible people who have much to contribute. Even if we disagree with them or if they are demonstrably wrong, we treat them with respect. We avoid punitive behaviors, focusing instead on positive motivation contributing to their growth and development as people. We treat them as we would like to be treated if the roles were reversed. Good things happen when we take principles of adult education seriously.

When I taught a Bible-story-plus-discussion approach to African pastors, I asked them to use the method in their church and report what happened. One reported,

> *My church is composed primarily of illiterate farmers. I told them the Bible story and had them retell it. Then I asked them questions about it and they answered. When I asked whether they had any questions, they asked questions that I could not answer. I realized that although they are uneducated, my church members are quite intelligent. If I do this again, I will have to prepare better.*

His respect for his church members grew when he treated them as adult learners and discovered that they were more capable than he knew. It is amazing what can happen as we shift to teaching and learning approaches that heed what we know about adult learners.

Back to institutional change. It may be possible in some institutions to alter what they are doing in one sweeping set of changes. It is more likely given the nature of theological institutions, that changes will come over a period of time in a more incremental manner. Incremental change seems woven into the culture of academia. If wholesale changes are not possible, we need not grow frustrated. Instead, we can implement and advocate for piecemeal improvements. Change within institutions may follow a sequence such as the following:

- Individual faculty members catch the vision for using more oral methods in their classes and begin to make changes within the courses they already teach. They make these changes while staying within the course description provided by the institution and pursuing the learning outcomes that are mutually agreed upon for that course. Irving, Moon, and Motty gave numerous examples of this. They help some of their more innovative colleagues to do likewise.

- Interested faculty members advocate within their institution for adding a course or additional courses about orality and oral strategies. These courses may focus on Bible storytelling, the use of indigenous art forms in worship, cross-cultural communication, and so forth. (James Krabill's discussion of lessons from the locally-originated African churches he has studied stimulated questions about contextualization and the threat of syncretism. This is an issue that David Sills raised as well in his responses to Moon, Motty, and Mark Overstreet. He cautioned that in our enthusiasm over cultural insights and methodological innovations, we dare not fail to submit them to critical evaluation in light of scripture.)

Talking about orality in existing courses or creating a course on orality are steps forward, to be sure. But they are not substitutes for making the classroom experience and the curriculum more oral. Ideally a training program would do both. The discussion at the consultation reinforced my opinion that if only one were possible, it would be more transforming for students to see their teachers using oral approaches in the classroom, in chapel services, and in congregational ministry than simply to talk in the classroom about orality as a phenomenon of intellectual curiosity. Faculty members' effective modeling of oral methods in their own ministry is the most powerful endorsement of orality and oral methods.

- Existing theological education institutions may sponsor separate training programs to meet the needs of oral learners. An institution may incorporate many of these changes in training programs designed for students who would not normally be admissible to the major programs of the institution. These may be at the certificate level, for instance, or even something at a lower academic level than the certificate programs.

- Institutions may begin to rethink the whole make up of their curriculum or their degree programs preparing people for Christian ministry. They realize that the traditional division of the curriculum is not the only way that one might teach such matter to people preparing for ministry. For example, why is it that biblical studies are typically taught separate from preaching? The typical division of the curriculum that is found in Western and Western-influenced seminaries is but one way of slicing the pie. It reflects an analytical approach that may not be the best in oral cultures.

In fact, given what is commonly thought about oral cultures, a more integrative approach to curriculum seems advisable for students who live in an oral culture with its holistic and integrative way of looking at life. An intermediate step toward greater integration could be for institutions to have selected courses team taught. Damon So has argued that oral biblical storytelling can be an excellent way to bring together biblical studies and systematic theology, two disciplines that frequently do not interact enough with one another.

- Hand-in-hand with changes to curriculum, which then leads to other changes within the theological education environment, institutions will need to be in dialogue with the accrediting bodies for theological education in their country or their region. It does us no good to ignore the influence that accrediting agencies have. When they function well, they can play a critically important role in helping institutions achieve their stated purposes in ways that show wisdom in governance, integrity in academic programs, and stability in finances. Accrediting agencies can be forces for change, as the practices found in the healthiest and most vibrant institutions are made available to other institutions accredited by that same accrediting body.

It seems farfetched to imagine that an accrediting body would ever accredit a diploma or degree program that did not include reading, research, and writing as cornerstone components. Those skills are so ingrained in our understanding of what education is that it is unrealistic to go to accrediting agencies asking them to accredit a diploma or degree that does not include them. But what institutions can do in dialogue with their accrediting agency is to look for appropriate ways to assess and accredit degrees that give a more prominent place to oral means of acquiring knowledge, changing attitudes and values, and developing skills. We need ways to evaluate both the intake through oral means in learning and the expression of that learning through oral means.

The academic world already includes diplomas and degrees that are more like this than typical theological education. For example, if a student gets a degree in piano performance, the performance skills are not evaluated by written exam. To demonstrate proficiency in piano performance, the student must perform at the piano. The appropriate evaluation for that part of the degree is to assess the performance itself. Likewise, a degree in theater arts with an emphasis in acting should make ample place within its assessment to evaluate the students' actual performance as actors. The playing of the role in a live situation with an audience is the natural expression of a degree in acting. So it stands to reason that such a degree ought to be evaluated in its performance dimension and that the degree ought not to be granted just on the basis of the students' ability to read, research, and write about the theater.

Likewise, community colleges and technical colleges offer a wide variety of one-year and two-year programs of study that combine classroom learning based upon reading, note taking, and written exams with a very substantial amount of learning through hands-on practice of the skills involved. Such programs can be very demanding and produce students with a high degree of achievement in these technical fields.

Appropriate assessment in these programs includes some written work and written evaluations in addition to a substantial amount of evaluation based upon the students' actual performance of the skills in a simulated work environment or actual on-the-job performance.

It is not difficult to imagine how a theological institution could assess many more elements of the actual practice of ministry. The assessment of students' learning could include many oral elements, from preaching and teaching, to storytelling, to counseling (including the use of traditional art forms like proverbs and parables), to music. Oral examinations could be the norm rather than the exception. Student presentations could be offered as alternatives to written exams and research papers as vehicles for demonstrating student learning.

The preceding discussion assumes that theological institutions recognize that adequate preparation of students for ministry does involve substantial attention to skill in ministry. It assumes that theological institutions do not see themselves simply as dealing in the intellectual and academic realm of students' preparation.

It may be that there are theological institutions that do see their work as primarily if not exclusively in the cognitive, intellectual, and academic dimensions. It is not surprising that institutions which see this as their purpose may be slower to include orality as a guiding principle in their curriculum design. There are still theological education institutions which look to the universities—and actually selected departments within universities—for their model. If faculty members have been trained in universities where the focus is almost entirely on intellectual development, then they may find it difficult to adjust to the kind of seminary program that this book is recommending. But we should challenge them, encourage them, and assist them as they dream what theological education per se should be.

It is often fruitful to involve members of the theological faculty in discussions about the actual purpose of theological education. Who is its rightful constituency? Theological institutions naturally focus on preparing graduates who will serve the existing churches that support the institution. If seminaries fail to do that, the churches may withdraw support and the seminary may collapse. But if the Bible college or seminary sees its mission as merely providing clergy for existing congregations, it takes too narrow a view of the rightful role of such entities in the Kingdom of God.

The faculty and administration of such institutions, in dialogue with their constituents, need always to keep clearly before them the need to prepare students who will begin new congregations and who will reach into segments of society that are not already part of the existing constituency.

I have led such dialogues with faculty members from a number of established theological education institutions. I am glad to report that in those discussions, although faculty members often defended the status quo and advocated making their institutions more academically rigorous, when I pressed this issue, they admitted that they entered teaching at a seminary or Bible college not primarily to be an academic specialist in a narrow field but because they wanted to see the Kingdom of God advance.

They were willing to acknowledge that the Kingdom of God is greatly advanced when the gospel goes to those who have never heard, and healthy, biblically-based congregations emerge as the tangible embodiment of the gospel in communities that had not previously known it. The faculty members with whom I have had this kind of discussion do typically say their calling is a gospel-focused calling; their calling is not typically to be an academic specialist in a single discipline within the curriculum.

If, however, an institution has recruited a faculty full of such persons, the changes we are talking about here could be exceedingly difficult to implement. But I am hopeful that the vast majority of theological educators are responsive to an appeal of this sort.

More often than not, faculty members are willing to make changes in new non-degree programs before they begin to remake the existing degree programs. That is an understandable approach. Phil Walker, however, appealed to leaders in theological education not to push orality to non-degree programs, lest oral approaches become relegated to the margins of theological education. He insisted that orality is too important in transforming students' lives for it to be kept in only some programs of study.

With the wide array of suggestions offered and the encouragement of colleagues who are interested in serving oral learners more effectively, we look to the years ahead with expectancy. Innovative informal training will continue to influence formal theological education. Training models developed where the Church is in its infancy will filter back to established institutions. Success in one place opens doors in another. Change is coming—change that will benefit oral learners and advance the Kingdom of God to God's glory.

Participants' Biographies

Miriam Adeney (PhD, anthropology) is author of *Kingdom without Borders: The Untold Story of Global Christianity* and other books. Professor at Seattle Pacific University and Regent College, Miriam serves on the board of *Christianity Today*, the mission commission of the World Evangelical Alliance, and the diaspora task force of the Lausanne Movement. She is past President of the American Society of Missiology.

Lon Allison is Executive Director of the Billy Graham Center at Wheaton College, where he directs a comprehensive team that seeks to "accelerate global evangelism." He is also Associate Professor of Evangelism and Leadership at Wheaton College Graduate School.

Jackson Atkins is President of Discipleship Multiplication Int. He teaches people worldwide how to implement oral methods, including setting up oral Bible schools. He has taught oral strategies in seminary and specializes in training leaders to teach others how to incorporate oral methods in ministry.

Peter Au (PhD, Dallas Theological Seminary) is Principal of the Canadian Chinese School of Theology at Tyndale University College and Seminary and is Director of Educational Projects International, Send International. He is also Consultant Pastor of Richmond Hill Christian Community Church.

Scott Barfoot (ThM, PhD) is Director of Dallas Theological Seminary's *Doctor of Ministry program*. Scott aspires to equip and empower global ministry leaders who impact the next generation for the cause of Christ. He and his wife, Debbie, of 15 years have three children, David, Joel, and Karissa.

Gary Bekker (MDiv., Calvin Theological Seminary; PhD, Michigan State University) is Director of Christian Reformed World Missions. He served as a missionary in the Philippines, and on the faculties of Gordon-Conwell and Calvin Theological Seminaries, where he also served as Academic Dean. His research interests include face-to-face interaction in intercultural settings and curriculum research for adult non-formal education.

Linda Bemis is Prayer Director for International Orality Network. She is focused on prayer being foundational, spirit-driven, and kingdom-oriented. She also works to bring awareness of the need for prayer advocates for Unengaged Unreached People Groups and those working in orality/UUPGs and Great Commission partner groups.

William Bjorakar is Associate Professor of Judeo-Christian Studies and Contemporary Western Culture at William Carey International University (WCIU) in Pasadena, California. He and his wife were missionaries in Israel through the 1980s. He is a U.S. missionary to Jewish people of Los Angeles under the Assemblies of God, and uses Bible storytelling in Jewish ministry.

Darryl Bowe serves as Vice President of International Operations for International Christian Ministries, helping to manage relationships with partnering ministries in Africa. He holds an MA in New Testament Theology and is working on a PhD in Orality and Theological Education at SATS.

Sarah Chae is a graduate student at Columbia University exploring the field of narrative medicine.

Samuel Chiang is Executive Director of the International Orality Network. Samuel serves the Church through writing, discipling, and exploring implementable orality strategies. A graduate of Dallas Seminary, he is passionate about faith and work. Samuel and Roberta and their three children have lived in Hong Kong for 22 years.

Emmanuel Chemengich is an ordained Anglican minister from Kenya and serves as Principal of Africa Theological Seminary (ATS) based in Kitale, Kenya, and with campuses in Uganda, Tanzania, Burundi, and D.R. Congo. ATS is committed to integrating orality approaches into all its study programs.

Scott Cunningham is passionate about global evangelical theological education. He has worked in more formal educational settings over the last 30 years: teaching in Nigerian seminaries, overseeing accreditation for African seminaries, and is now with Overseas Council. As a member of SIM, he places a high value on leadership development for the Church through multiple models.

Steve Evans has been a communications specialist and cultural researcher since 1982. He studied at Howard Payne University, Southwestern Baptist Theological Seminary, and East Tennessee State University. He is the 2008 recipient of the prestigious Brimstone Award for Applied Storytelling and has published extensively on the topic of orality. Steve lives in London.

Jason Ferenczi is Program Officer for Leadership Development at Cornerstone Trust in Grand Rapids. Prior to beginning this role in March 2012, Jason served for 14 years with Overseas Council in Indianapolis, most recently as Vice President. He and Stefanii have four daughters.

Joyce Gibson is an intercessor for various ministries.

Bill Goold is the Dwight M. and Lucille S. Beeson Professor of Church Music and the William Earle Edwards Professor of Church Music at Asbury Seminary. Bill received a BA in Bible and Theology from Vennard College, a BME and MM in Vocal Performance from Drake University, and a DMA in Vocal Pedagogy from the University of Kentucky.

Chandler Im (PhD, Fuller Theological Seminary) is Director of Ethnic Ministries at the Billy Graham Center at Wheaton College. He is also the Director of Ethnic America Network, a coalition of 70-plus evangelical denominations and mission agencies in the USA and Canada. Currently, he is co-editing *Global Diasporas and Mission* (Regnum, forthcoming).

David Irving is 54 years old and married with two teenage children. He is a U.S. citizen who works as a missionary with Youth with a Mission in Labrea, Amazon state, Brazil. He has been in Brazil for 25 years, working with indigenous people groups for 24 of those.

James R. Krabill (PhD, University of Birmingham, U.K.) has served with Mennonite missions since 1976 in France, England, and West Africa. For half that time he was a Bible and church history instructor among African-initiated churches, primarily in Cote d'Ivoire. A writer/editor of numerous publications, he recently completed an ethnodoxology handbook, *Worship and Mission for the Global Church* (2013).

Robert Kurka is Professor of Theology and Church in Culture at Lincoln Christian University, Lincoln, Illinois. He is a regular Perspectives lecturer and is a contributor to the new Wipf & Stock text, *River of God*, edited by Stephen Burris and Douglas D. Priest.

Chuck Lawless (PhD) is Dean of Graduate Studies at Southeastern Seminary and Global Theological Education Consultant for the International Mission Board of the Southern Baptist Convention. Chuck and his wife, Pam, reside in Wake Forest, North Carolina.

Grant Lovejoy is Director of Orality Strategies for the International Mission Board. While a professor of preaching, hermeneutics, and Bible storying in the U.S., he co-developed theological training for oral learners in Sudan. He co-edited *Making Disciples of Oral Learners* and authored "That All May Hear" for Lausanne III. He writes for OralityStrategies.org.

Charles Madinger (DMin, Fuller Theological Seminary) invested 27 years in missional vocational ministry. He has taught at universities and seminaries in the U.S. and abroad and has launched three mission and consulting organizations helping to reach the oral majority with partners in over 20 countries. He is now completing a PhD in Communication at the University of Kentucky.

Stephen Mairori is the International Coordinator of International Christian Ministries (ICM) and also Executive Director of ICM Kenya. He chairs the Governing Council of Africa Theological Seminary in Kenya and has served as a pastor and ordained minister in the Africa Inland Church Kenya for more than 20 years. Stephen earned a MDiv from Fresno Pacific Seminary. He is married to Roselyne and has three children.

Ed Meadors is Professor of Biblical Studies at Taylor University. He has a PhD from the University of Aberdeen, an MA from Wheaton College Graduate School, and a BA from Wheaton College.

Dorothy Miller is Executive Director of The God's Story Project, scriptwriter of its flagship tool, "God's Story: From Creation to Eternity" (now in 300 languages). Dorothy develops storytelling tools, including "Simply the Story," an oral-style inductive Bible study used in 90 countries and 60 oral Bible schools.

Roland Moody retired from Macy's in Atlanta, Georgia, as Divisional Vice President. He has traveled the world, entering China in 1978 after it was opened. He worked as Vice President of Communications for The Haggai Institute in charge of the website, videos, books, marketing collateral, and meetings held around the world.

W. Jay Moon is Professor of Intercultural Studies and Director of the Wesley House of Study at Sioux Falls Seminary. From 1992-2001, he was a SIM missionary among the primarily oral Builsa people in Ghana, West Africa. His two books, *African Proverbs Reveal Christianity in Culture* and *Ordinary Missionary*, highlight orality.

Scott Moreau served for ten years (Swaziland/Kenya) with Campus Crusade for Christ in Africa, leaving in 1991 to teach at Wheaton College Graduate School. He is Professor of Intercultural Studies and Associate Dean of Wheaton Graduate School, Editor of *Evangelical Missions Quarterly*, and General Editor of the *Encountering Mission* series (Baker).

Bauta Motty is Professor of Leadership and Missions, ECWA Theological Seminary, Jos, Plateau State, Nigeria. Born at Ambam Kaninkon, he is married to Deborah with four children. A pastor/teacher with Evangelical Church Willing All (ECWA) since 1976, he served as General Secretary of ECWA and a Member of the Government Judicial Commission of Inquiry.

Mark Overstreet serves as Vice President for T4Global. He serves with a passion for global missions, ministry, and leadership. From the seminary classroom to mud huts around the world among oral cultures, he teaches pastors in leadership development, church planting, discipleship, and evangelism. Additionally, he consults with organizations in areas including orality, theology, discipleship, and communication strategy.

Tom Phillips serves with the Billy Graham Evangelistic Association and is Vice President, overseeing the Billy Graham Library

M. David Sills is Associate Dean of Christian Missions and Professor of Christian Missions and Cultural Anthropology at The Southern Baptist Theological Seminary, as well as President of Reaching & Teaching International Ministries. David served as a missionary in Ecuador as well as in pastoral leadership development around the world.

Jeff Singerman (MDiv, Mid-America Baptist Theological Seminary) was appointed a career missionary with the International Mission Board in 1989. Jeff ministered in Benin as a student worker, church planter, and presently leads the Assist team that works closely with partnering African Francophone conventions. He is currently pursuing a PhD at Southeastern Seminary.

Damon So is Research Tutor in Theology at the Oxford Centre for Mission Studies. He is author of *The Forgotten Jesus and the Trinity You Never Knew* (Wipf and Stock, 2010), and *Jesus' Revelation of His Father: A Narrative-Conceptual Study of the Trinity with Special Reference to Karl Barth* (Paternoster, 2006).

David Swarr (PhD) serves as President and CEO of Davar Partners International, a scripture engagement organization. David is passionate about the role of audio scriptures in transforming oral communities. He grew up in the Middle East and has lived and served on five continents. He has a rich background in cross-cultural leadership, including senior positions in multinational companies, NGOs, and at an university.

Tom Steffen served 20 years with New Tribes Mission, 15 in the Philippines. He is Professor of Intercultural Studies in the Cook School of Intercultural Studies at Biola University, California, where he directs the DMiss program. His latest book is *The Facilitator Era: Beyond Pioneer Church Multiplication.*

LaNette Thompson and her husband pioneered the use of Chronological Bible Storying in West Africa for the International Mission Board. After 26 years in missions, they now reside in Texas, where she is in the PhD program in Educational Psychology at Baylor University. Five of her grandchildren serve with their parents in Africa.

Phil Thornton (PhD, cultural anthropology) is Chair of the Resource team for COSIM, and an international teacher for Global Impact Missions. He served as missionary in Latin America, and taught as professor of missions at Asbury University.

Mary Verghese (PhD, education) is a retired professor and research guide. She is a board member of New India Evangelistic Association (NIEA) and a consultant for Curriculum Development and Research with New India Bible Seminary (NIBS), the training wing of NIEA. She is passionate to transform the Bible-less communities of India through proclamation and demonstration of the word of God.

Phil Walker (PhD, education) has served with his wife in the Middle East and Africa. Phil is President of International Christian Ministries—USA and Chancellor of Africa Theological Seminary.

Acknowledgement

A mini-global consultation with a short ramp-up time requires a host of supporters, encouragers, and experimenters. Furthermore, to bring the presentations into a quartet of book, audio, video, and web presence requires dedicated and passionate souls who are already on the journey. We would like to thank Laurie Nichols for superb editing, thoughtful comments, and guiding us where we need to go with this publication. We also are thankful to the teams who were instrumental in making this dream a reality:

Programming Team: Samuel Chiang, Grant Lovejoy, Charles Madinger, Mark Overstreet, Roland Moody, and David Swarr

Communications, Design, and Edit Team: Joni Chiang, Jan Dantone, Anneli Deacon, Yvonne Lam, Nancy Lucenay, Cindy Morris, Ivan Ng, Ivy Shum, and Sandra Zee

Hosting Team: Lon Allison, Jean Bilang, Troy Bristow, and Sarah Chae

Audio, Video, and Technology Team: Micah Chiang, Phil Thornton, Joseph Vijayam and the thoroughly professional and caring technologists at OliveTech.com; Bryan Thompson who provided the audio version of this book, which can be accessed at: story4all.libsyn.com/.

Electronic Publishing Team: Sarah O'Neal, Owner/Designer, Eve Custom Artwork and Brent Lindquist, Publisher, CondeoPress

Resources Team: A special thank you to discreet, anonymous investors in the USA and Hong Kong, who gave passionately to Kingdom work and to this event, as well as making this book come alive.

The birthing of this mini-global consultation and subsequent book and materials could not have taken place without the work of prayer, creating the invisible foundation and platform for us to meet, hear, and collaborate. We wish to thank Linda Bemis, Joyce Gibson, and a core of intercessors, all of whom fasted and prayed for all those months prior to and post the actual consultation.

To God be the glory!

Glossary

(These terms and definitions have been gathered from a variety of sources, including our flagship books, *Making Disciples of Oral Learners* and *Orality Breakouts: Using Heart Language to Transform Hearts*. This is not an exhaustive list and the definitions are not universally agreed upon.)

Andragogy: The art and science of helping adults learn. The term was popularized in an attempt to develop a theory specifically for adult learning in contrast with theories for children's learning.

Audio Bible: Audio recordings of intact units of scripture that come verbatim from an accepted translation of the Bible. Most often, these are recordings of an entire book of the Bible or the New Testament, but some audio Bibles are comprised of selections of other kinds, such as biblical psalms or stories. Not to be confused with an oral Bible. See "oral Bible."

Bible storying: A generic term which includes the many forms of telling Bible stories. Sometimes, it includes Chronological Bible Storying (CBS), but can refer to the use of Bible storytelling in non-chronological ways, such as single stories related to ministry needs, thematic story clusters in teaching and preaching, and storytelling, which begins with the story of Jesus according to the local need and strategy.

Broad sowing: An evangelistic or media approach to provide spiritual content to a large audience.

Chronological Bible Storying (CBS): A method of sharing biblical truths by telling the stories of the Bible as intact stories in the order they happened in time. The person using this method leads the hearers to discover the truths in the stories for the purpose of evangelization, discipleship, church planting, and leader training. Jim Slack and J. O. Terry developed CBS when they saw the need for a purely oral approach to oral peoples. CBS is promoted globally by IMB (International Mission Board of the Southern Baptist Convention).

Chronological Bible Storytelling: The act of presenting biblical truth in story format—although the story may be deeply paraphrased or interrupted for elaboration when an important issue occurs in the passage. The story may or may not be kept intact as a story. It follows a chronologically-organized timeline.

Communication preference: The favored style or method of communication for an individual or group of people. There are two dominant poles in a communication preference continuum—oral and literate—and major differences between literate or print-oriented communicators and oral communicators in the way they receive and communicate information. See "literate communicator" and "oral communicator."

Crafting a story, story crafting: Shaping the stories from a literature format to an oral format and making the changes needed to maintain a clear focus on the story's main point(s), to give clarity in telling, to adapt to certain worldview issues, and to provide story continuity leading to the storying track objective of evangelism, discipling, leader training, etc. *Oralizing Bible Stories for Telling* by J. O. Terry discusses a variety of approaches to story crafting.

Functional illiterate/functional illiteracy: UNESCO has recommended the following definition: "A person is functionally illiterate who cannot engage in all those activities in which literacy is required for effective functioning of his group and community, and also for enabling him to continue to use reading, writing and calculation for his own and the community's development." A person who has had some education, but does not meet a minimum standard of literacy. The person reads poorly and without adequate understanding and lacks sufficient skills in literacy to function as a literate person in his or her society. Some statistics indicate that 70 percent of the world's population is either illiterate or functionally illiterate. See "illiterate" for comment on usage.

Heart language: See "mother tongue."

Illiterate: Not able to read and write. See "functional" and "oral preference."

Literate: The person is literate who, in a language that he or she speaks, can read and understand anything he or she would have understood if it had been spoken, and who can write anything that he or she can speak so that it can be read.

Literate communicator: One whose preferred or most effective communication or learning method is in accordance with literate formats. Literate format or style expresses itself through analytic, sequential, and linear thought patterns. Many missionaries are literate communicators trying to reach oral communicators. See "oral communicator."

Mother tongue: A person's first language; a person's native language learned from birth; the language of the hearth and home; a person's heart language; the language a person understands best; the language of fear, grief, joy, love, devotion, and intimacy; the cherished language learned in infancy between mother and child.

Non-literate: An alternative, less-pejorative term for "illiterate." See "illiterate."

Oral Bible: The term is used *descriptively* to refer to the knowledge of scripture that people acquire by oral and aural means. These means include hearing sermons preached, lessons taught, scripture read aloud, the Bible quoted, Bible stories told, biblical lyrics sung, audio recordings of scripture played, and more. An oral Bible thus is a potpourri of biblical knowledge coming from many oral and aural sources. An oral Bible consists of only what can be remembered, so each person's oral Bible will be different from that of another person and will change with time and exposure. When Christian workers recognized that oral learners live by what they can remember from the Bible, they decided to develop an oral process to help oral learners get a more accurate, complete, and cohesive knowledge of scripture. Chronological Bible Storying, for example, was developed in part to provide an orderly, cohesive, and memorable knowledge of scripture to oral learners. In that context, the term "oral Bible" was often used *prescriptively* (e.g., "We are giving them an 'oral Bible.'") The term is less frequently used in some circles today because it was often confused with "audio Bible." See "audio Bible."

Oral communicator: A person who learns or processes information by spoken rather than literate means. Some oral communicators are so out of necessity because they cannot read or read with understanding. Other oral communicators can read with understanding and write, but they prefer non-print forms of communication.

Oral learner: A person whose mental framework is primarily influenced by spoken rather than literate forms of communication and who therefore learns primarily or exclusively by speech, song, etc.

Oral preference: A predilection for communicating or receiving and processing information using spoken means rather than print. The term may apply to non-readers as well as readers, but it is often used to refer to people who are able to read with understanding but who are predisposed to spoken communication for cultural or aesthetic reasons. See "oral communicator."

Orality: The quality or state of being oral. The habitual ways of thought and spoken communication that are characteristic of cultures where most people are unfamiliar with the technology of literacy, especially writing and print. The constellation of characteristics (cognitive, communicational, and relational) typical of cultures that function orally. See www.oralitystrategies.org/strategy_detail.cfm?StrategyID=1&start=3.

People group: A significantly large grouping of individuals who perceive themselves to have a common affinity for one another because of their shared language, religion, ethnicity, residence, occupation, class or caste, situation, or combinations of these. For evangelistic purposes, the largest group within which the gospel can spread as a church-planting movement without encountering barriers of understanding or acceptance.

Primary oral culture: A culture with no knowledge of writing.

Primary orality: The state of persons totally unfamiliar with writing. People who have never seen a word.

Residual orality: Thought and its verbal expression in cultures that have been exposed to writing and print, but have not fully "interiorized" (Marshall McLuhan's term) and the use of these technologies in their daily lives. An educated elite who are competent in literacy can co-exist alongside the majority of the population who live by the speech-based forms of communication that pre-date the introduction of literacy. "Residual orality" is sometimes referred to as "traditional orality."

Secondary orality: Orality that is delivered by electronic media and which depends upon writing and print for its existence; technologized orality. Contrasted with "primary orality" (see above). Radio, television, and other electronic media utilize traditional forms of oral communication, such as storytelling and songs; however, electronic media usually separates the literate creators and performers from their audience by geography and by time, so secondary orality is seldom face-to-face oral communication. The habits of thought and communication made possible by literacy shape secondary orality.

Story crafting: See "crafting a story/story crafting."

Story fellowship groups: Gatherings to teach, learn, and practice Bible stories and how to apply them (theologically, pastorally, socially, etc.) in a relevant way; works well with all oral preference learners from primary oral to secondary oral learners.

Storying: The term "storying" is an attempt to make a strong statement about the value of the intact, uninterrupted Bible narrative as a valuable means of teaching God's word leading to salvation, church planting, discipling, leader training, and various ministry activities. Storying is not limited in purpose to teaching non-literates. It is used because it is reproducible by listeners and because the use of story helps to overcome resistance or hostility to traditional westernized teaching. See "Chronological Bible Storying."

Unreached people group (UPG): More broadly, an ethnic group which does not possess a church and which does not have the presence of an indigenous Christian witness. A people, usually an ethnolinguistic group, with an historical culture, language, and often a geographical place of residence where there is little or no presence of evangelical Christianity, especially in the forms of Bible, Christian gospel presentations, believers, baptisms, and churches. A people group within which there is no indigenous community of believing Christians to evangelize this people group without requiring outside (cross-cultural) assistance. A people group in which less than 2 percent of the population are evangelical Christians. A group is considered "reached" if it has a viable, indigenous, self-reproducing church movement in its midst.

Worldview: The way a specific people perceives and makes sense of the world around them. Somewhat like wearing tinted lenses, members of a culture look *through* their worldview, not *at* it. A worldview is seldom apparent to its adherents unless it comes under question. A worldview consists of fundamental cognitive, affective, and evaluative assumptions about reality. A worldview forms the core of a culture, which guides people in how to act, think, believe, function, and relate. How people look at life and the world around them; a people's view of the world. A profile of the way people within a specified culture live, act, think, work, and relate.

Annotated Bibliography

The following first appeared in the book *Orality Breakouts* published by ION/ Lausanne. The condensed list of selected books, journals, and websites has been updated to include the most current information (all URL links were last accessed March 13, 2013).

Books

Adeney, Miriam. 2002. *Daughters of Islam: Building Bridges with Muslim Women*. Downers Grove, IL: InterVarsity Press.
Insights on how to relate to Muslim women by exploring aspects of their daily life such as family, children, religious practice, and finances. Knowledge of these things provides a framework for acquainting them with Christ.

_____. 2009. *Kingdom Without Borders: The Untold Story of Global Christianity*. Downers Grove, IL: InterVarsity Press.
Adeney shares the personal stories of Christians from all over the globe, including their faith, struggles, and perseverance. This book removes us from our sheltered lives and calls us to reach out and extend our faith to beyond our day-to-day surroundings.

Bailey, Kenneth E. 1983. *Poet & Peasant and Through Peasant Eyes: A Literary-Cultural Approach to the Parables in Luke*. Combined ed. Grand Rapids, MI: William B. Eerdmans Publishing Co.
Bailey analyzes parables in the Gospel of Luke through both literary and cultural means. Having worked within Middle Eastern peasant culture over the past two decades, he provides excellent insight on the cultural assumptions of these parables.

Barrett, David. 1990. *Our Globe and How to Reach It*. Birmingham, AL: New Hope.
Classic reference book.

Bauerlein, Mark. 2008. *The Dumbest Generation: How the Digital Age Stupifies Young Americans and Jeopardizes Our Future*. New York: Penguin.

Bradshaw, Tom and Bonnie Nichols. 2010. *Reading at Risk: A Survey of Literary Reading in America, Research Division Report # 46. National Endowment for the Arts 2004*. Available from www.arts.gov/pub/readingatrisk.pdf.

Cannell, Linda. 2006. *Theological Education Matters*. eprinted by Edcot Press.

Coe, John. 2012. *Metamorpha*. 'The Abiding Life' Conference.

Carruthers, Mary. 2008. *The Book of Memory: A Study of Memory in Medieval Culture*. 2nd ed. New York: Cambridge University Press.
This book has transformed the way modern scholars view medieval culture by examining the role of memory—namely *trained* memory. It is a must-read for anyone interested in orality, literacy, memory, or meditation.

Chiang, Samuel and Steve Evans, eds. 2010. *Orality Breakouts: Using Heart Language to Transform Hearts*. International Orality Network and the Lausanne Congress on World Evangelization.
These global case studies work to demonstrate the *how* of using an oral-based approach to reach the multitude of people who learn scripture and gospel content through such methods.

Chomsky, Noam. 2000. *New Horizons in the Study of Language and Mind*. Cambridge: Cambridge University Press.
A must-read for anyone interested in the subject of language. A fresh perspective on old issues and questions.

Collins, Rives. 2005. *The Power of a Story*. Long Grove, IL: Waveland Press, Inc. Collins raises the question of why we should tell stories—and *how*. It provides pointers on the *how*, as well as activities that can be used in a classroom setting, enriching people's learning through storytelling.

Cranton, Patricia. 1992. *Working with Adult Learners*. Toronto: Wall & Emerson.

Crouch, Andy. 2008. *Culture Making: Recovering Our Creative Calling*. Downers Grove, IL: InterVarsity Press.
Crouch calls Christians not to condemn or change culture, but to *create* culture. He examines the different facets of culture, providing us with knowledge of how to cultivate our own in partnership with God.

Dagron, Alfonso Gumucio. 2001. *Making Waves: Stories of Participatory Communication for Social Change*. New York: The Rockefeller Foundation.
A collection of case studies showing the usage of media and arts working with relevant worldview and heart language to affect change.

Day, Jackson. 2007. *Bible Storytelling Tools: A Guide for Storying the Bible*. La Vergne, TN: Lightning Source.
A resource book that assists teachers in communicating biblical stories orally. It explains the strengths of oral communication as well as why some people prefer it to reading.

DeNeui, Paul H., ed. 2008. *Communicating Christ through Story and Song: Orality in Buddhist Contexts*. Pasadena, CA: William Carey Library.
The latest volume in the Buddhist World series holds models and case studies of gospel communication through oral means in Southeast Asia. It showcases the importance of oral tradition as a way to effectively communicate in a Buddhist context, helping us learn how we might witness to Buddhists.

Denning, Stephen. 2005. *The Leader's Guide to Storytelling*. San Francisco: Jossey-Bass.
Denning addresses how to tell the right story at the right time, maximizing the story's effect on the audience in doing so.

Dillon, Christine. 2012. *Telling the Gospel Through Story: Evangelism that Keeps Hearers Wanting More*. Downers Grove, IL: InterVarsity Press.
Dillon shares her discovery that biblical storytelling is far more effective than other evangelistic approaches. She provides tips for how to deliver such stories and lead discussions on them, and how to evangelize while doing so.

Donovan, Vincent J. 1978. *Christianity Rediscovered*. Maryknoll, N.Y.: Orbis.
Donovan was a Catholic missioner working in Kenya who tried to teach the
people traditional material, but soon discovered that they were oral people who
were more receptive to Bible stories. He writes on the knowledge he gained.

Engel, James. 1977. *How Can I Get Them to Listen?* Grand Rapids, MI:
Zondervan.
An old classic that may still be found in libraries.

Ford, Leighton. 1994. *The Power of Story. Rediscovering the Oldest, Most Natural
Way to Reach People for Christ*. Colorado Springs, CO: NavPress.
The author describes how the best way to witness to others is also the oldest and
purest way—the way that Jesus, his followers, and the rest of the early evangelists
went out to share the good news.

Forest, Heather. 1996. *Wisdom Tales from Around the World*. Atlanta, GA:
August House.
A global collection of folklore and stories from across different religious and
cultural background with the author making observations about the wisdom
from the stories.

Foster, Richard. 1978, 1988. *Celebration of Discipline: The Path to Spiritual
Growth*. New York: Harper Collins Publishers.

_____. 1993. *Devotional Classics*. San Francisco: Harpercollins.

Fortunato, Frank, with Paul Neeley and Carol Brinneman. 2006. *All the World
Is Singing: Glorifying God through the Worship Music of the Nations*. Tyrone, GA/
Bucks, U.K.: Authentic.
These stories bear witness to the power of music in evangelism and worship—
especially in the far reaches of the earth, where indigenous peoples are
encouraged to give their songs to the Lord.

Finnegan, Ruth. 2007. *The Oral and Beyond: Doing Things with Words in Africa*.
Oxford: James Curry Ltd.
Finnegan examines how people use words to describe their surroundings and link
past to present. This is a valuable book for historians, linguists, anthropologists,
and anyone interested in culture.

Furniss, Graham. 2004. *Orality. The Power of the Spoken Word*. Basingstoke:
Palgrave Macmillan.
The written word is considered one of the most powerful forms of
communication; however, in this book, the spoken word is dubbed worthy to
contend with literature, as it holds great communicative influence as well.

Gardner, Howard. 1993. *Multiple Intelligences: the Theory and Practice*. New
York: Basicbooks.

_____. 2006. *Multiple Intelligences: New Horizons in Theory and Practice*.
New York: Basic Books.
Gardner's work provides foundational thinking for the modern classroom,
evaluations, rubrics, and portfolios.

Geurts, Kathryn Linn. 2002. *Culture and the Senses. Bodily Ways of Knowing in an African Community*. Berkeley: University of California Press.
While the West is familiar with the concept of five senses, this book reveals a culture that regards senses entirely differently. A unique perspective on sense and perception.

Godin, Seth. 2005. *All Marketers Are Liars: The Power of Telling Authentic Stories in a Low-Trust World*. New York: Portfolio.
Successful marketing is done through good storytelling—but whether or not the stories are authentic is the question. This book helps those interested in marketing know what makes a good (and not fraudulent) story that will sell.

Goody, Jack. 1968. *Literacy in Traditional Societies*. Cambridge: Cambridge University Press.
Social structures and changes in the African context are explained. Although the book is out of print, the book's observation of social changes, urbanization, and information technologies is still relevant for understanding societies in Africa.

Haven, Kendall. 2012. *Story Proof: The Science behind the Startling Power of Story*. Westport, CT: Libraries Unlimited.
An important contribution to knowledge about stories and why they work from a science perspective.

Hayes, Tom. 2008. *Jump Point: How Network Culture Is Revolutionizing Business*. New York: McGraw-Hill.
In a new age of worldwide connectedness, this guide prompts the reader to challenge old assumptions and redesign old business tactics in order to take advantage of this modern environment.

Heath, Chip and Dan Heath. 2007. *Made to Stick: Why Some Ideas Survive and Others Die*. New York: Random House.
This book examines why some ideas are successful and others are not and serves as a good guide on how to communicate ideas in such a way that they "stick" to our audience.

_____. 2010. *Switch: How to Change Things When Change is Hard*. New York: Broadway Books.
Change is something that might easily boost the numbers on anyone's blood pressure count; but this book is about how to deal with change and make it work to our advantage.

Hesselgrave, David. 1978. *Communicating Christ Cross-Culturally*. Grand Rapids, MI: Zondervan.
Hesselgrave examines literature on communication science to assist others carrying the gospel across cultures. He explains the role of culture in communication and contextualization. A great resource to have in churches and on campuses.

Hiebert, Paul. 1976. *Cultural Anthropology*. Grand Rapids, MI: Baker Book House.
An introduction to the subject of cultural anthropology from a Christian point of view.

_____. 1985. *Anthropological Insights for Missionaries*. Grand Rapids, MI: Baker Book House.
Hiebert appeals for the necessity of both scripture exegesis and human exegesis, the process of understanding the gospel, and the people to whom we take it.

_____. 2008. *Transforming Worldviews*. Grand Rapids, MI: Baker Book House.
Hiebert suggests that a change in worldview is essential to the confirmation of Christian conversion. He offers advice on how we may lead others to this shift in worldview, as well as explaining the nature of worldview itself.

Hipps, Shane. 2005. *The Hidden Power of Electronic Culture: How Media Shapes Faith, The Gospel, and Church*. Grand Rapids, MI: Zondervan.
As pop culture continues to thrive and new technology rapidly emerges, the Church is faced with the question of where it fits into the mix. The author examines this question as well as others that come up in the unearthing of an answer.

_____. 2009. *Flickering Pixels: How Technology Shapes Your Faith*. Grand Rapids, MI: Zondervan.
Hipps explains how technology in this modern age can easily impact the mind. He underlines the importance of being aware of what this impact is and how we can prevent technology from compromising our integrity.

Hirsh, Alan and Darryn Altclass. 2009. *The Forgotten Ways Handbook: a Practical Guide for Developing Missional Churches*. Grand Rapids, MI: Brazos Press.
In his last book, *The Forgotten Ways*, Hirsh wrote on how the modern Church could use power from the early Church for future growth. In this book, he sets this theory in motion by providing ways in which we can apply this idea.

Holt, David and Bill Mooney. 1996. *The Storyteller's Guide*. Little Rock, AR: August House.
Interviews with over 50 storytellers from a range of backgrounds serve as a guide to storytelling.

Howes, David. 2003. *Sensual Relations: Engaging the Senses in Culture and Social Theory*. Ann Arbor, MI: University of Michigan Press.
A wide-ranging, yet deep examination of sensory perception and cultural expression and how the two are interrelated.

Hubbard, Douglas W. 2010. *How to Measure Anything: Finding the Value of "Intangibles" in Business*. Hoboken, N.J.: John Wiley & Sons.
Anything can be measured—it's the *how* that poses the biggest problem to most people. In this book, Hubbard helps us answer the question of *how*, thereby helping us make better decisions.

Klem, Herbert. 1982. *Oral Communication of Scripture*. Pasadena, CA: William Carey Library.
Using insight from African oral art, the author argues oral communication strategies must be employed for the gospel to be heard and understood by the world of oral cultures.

Knowles, Malcolm S. 1980. *The Modern Practice of Adult Education*. Englewood Cliffs: Prentice Hall Regents.
A timeless book written ahead of its time.

Knowles, Malcolm and Associates. 1984. *Andragogy in Action*. San Francisco, CA: Jossey-Bass, Inc.
The author wrote the definitive book on adult learning.

Koehler, Paul F. 2010. *Telling God's Story with Power: Biblical Storytelling in Oral Cultures*. Pasadena, CA: William Cary Library.
Koehler introduces orality, explains biblical storytelling, and describes findings from case studies and research conducted among oral communities. To be read alongside of Christine Dillon's *Telling the Gospel Through Story*.

Krabill, James R., *The Hymnody of the Harrist Church among the Dida of South-Central Ivory Coast, 1913-1949*. Frankfurt: Peter Lang, 1995.
Difficult to find, but a treasure when found.

Krabill, James R., Frank Fortunato, Brian Schrag, Paul Neeley, and Robin Harris. 2012. *Ethnodoxology Handbook: Worship and Mission for the Global Church*. Pasadena, CA: William Cary Library.
A timely and timeless book for this new century—a must for every pastor's library.

LeFever, Marlene D. 1995. *Learning Styles: Reaching Everyone God Gave You to Teach*. Colorado Springs, CO: David C. Cook.
A classic for any Christian educator.

Levitin, Daniel J. 2008. *The World in Six Songs: How the Musical Brain Created Human Nature*. New York: Penguin Group (USA).
Music has shaped culture and society, and it is vastly important to the world today. Levitin breaks music down into six forms of song (friendship, joy, comfort, knowledge, religion, and love), and speaks on how these impact us globally.

Loewen, Jacob A. 1975. *Culture and Human Values*. Pasadena, CA: William Carey Library.
Loewen writes from a position of linguistic and cultural expertise. His chapter, "Bible Stories: Message and Matrix," is helpful for interaction with oral peoples.

Lovejoy, Grant, ed. 2005. *"Making Disciples of Oral Learners."* Lausanne Occasional Paper, no. 54 Bangalore: Lausanne Committee on World Evangelization and International Orality Network.
The formative work of the modern orality movement. It introduces the challenge of communicating the gospel to oral cultures, and provides the solution. It also explains the who, what, where, and why of the need for the orality movement. For more information, visit http://oralbible.com/workspace/resources/docs/Making_Disciples_of_Oral_Learners-1264691848.pdf.

McLuhan, Marshall. 1966. *Understanding Media: The Extensions of Man*. New York: McGraw-Hill, 1966.
McLuhan evaluates how culture and technology impact behavior in an age that enables us to be "plugged in" at all times. Oftentimes theoretical, this book examines our understanding of how and what we communicate.

Merriam, Sharan B., Caffarella, Rosemary S. & Baumgartner, Lisa M. 2007. *Learning in Adulthood*. San Francisco, CA: John Wiley & Sons.

Miller, Mark. 2003. *Experiential Storytelling: (Re)Discovering Narrative to Communicate God's Message*. Grand Rapids, MI: Zondervan.
How do we narrate good stories? And why? Miller writes to answer these questions and suggests that speaking from personal experience adds extra value to a story.

Moon, W. Jay. 2012. *Integrative Discipleship: Multi-cultural and Multi-generational Pedagogies for Worldview Transformation*. ASM series. Maryknoll, N.Y.: Orbis.
An informative read that is relevant to a range of cultures and generations.

_____. 2012. *Ordinary Missionary: A Narrative Approach to Introducing World Missions*. Eugene, OR: Resource Publications.
An excellent companion to W. Jay Moon's *Integrative Discipleship*.

Mottet, Timothy P., Virginia P. Richmond, and James C. McCorske. 2005. *Handbook of Instructional Communication: Rhetorical and Relational Perspectives*. Upper Saddle River, N.J.: Pearson.
Written by experts for designing learner-centered curriculum; a standard textbook in universities.

Mouton, Jane Srygley and Robert R. Blake. 1984. *Synergogy: A New Strategy for Education, Training and Development*. San Francisco: Jossey-Bass.

Newbigin, Lesslie. 1986. *Foolishness to the Greeks*. Grand Rapids, MI: William B. Eerdmans Publishing Co.
A classic by a missionary statesman, this landmark work challenges the reader to examine the issues raised in cross-cultural communication of the gospel and understand how a culture's great pillars (science, politics, and other sectors) should be confronted with the claims of the gospel.

Ngugi wa Thiong'o. 1986. *Decolonising the Mind. The Politics of Language in African Literature*. Oxford: James Currey.
A good read that points out the importance of specificity in communication and language.

Nicholls, Kathleen. 1983. *Asian Arts and Christian Hope*. New Delhi: Select Books.
This book examines how the good news may be spread through traditional arts.

Nida, Eugene. 1954, 1975. *Customs and Culture*. New York: Harper and Row. Reprint, Pasadena, CA: William Carey Library.
May be considered an older work, but still just as relevant.

_____. 1960. *Message and Mission: The Communication of the Christian Faith*. New York: Harper and Brothers.
With his experience as a Christian in the field of anthropology, Nida addresses the sociological theory in a way that makes it possible for us to engage other cultures with Christianity on a meaningful level.

Novelli, Michael. 2008. *Shaped by the Story: Helping Students Encounter God in a New Way*. Grand Rapids, Mi: Zondervan.
Novelli explores the significance of storytelling, and how it helps students experience God on a new level. He explains how theological knowledge imparted by storytelling can be more memorable, thereby providing students with a more solid foundation for their faith.

Ong, Walter J. 1982. *Orality and Literacy: The Technologizing of the Word*. London: Methuen.
This landmark work distinguishes orality and literacy and the cultures that embody the characteristics of each. Ong explores meaningful difference between oral and literate cultures and argues that oral communication transforms thought patterns, speech patterns, memory, and cultural consciousness.

Pagitt, Doug. 2005. *Preaching Re-Imagined*. Grand Rapids, MI: Zondervan.
What kind of communities are we forming? What story are we telling? How can we tell it more effectively? Pagitt addresses these questions of sociology, theology, and communications in order to help us engage the Bible meaningfully, which in turn encourages spiritual growth in the church community.

Peek, Philip M. and Yankah, Kwesi, eds. 2004. *African Folklore. An Encyclopedia*. New York: Routledge.
The first of its kind to cover such a detailed and in-depth range of African Folklore. It uncovers a wealth of information on cultures found in Africa.

Putman, Jim. 2009. *Church Is a Team Sport: A Championship Strategy for Doing Ministry Together*. Grand Rapids, MI: Baker Book House.
Highlights the importance of individual Christians making up the congregation. Putman shares his insight on how to make disciples out of people by investing time and care into them, in turn reflecting God's love.

_____. 2010. *Real-Life Discipleship: Building Churches that Makes Disciples*. Colorado Springs, CO: NavPress, 2010.
An important issue for spiritual leaders is how they can make disciples of others—and in a way that enables these new disciples to pass on their knowledge and do the same. Putman offers good strategies on how to do just this.

Putman, Jim, Brandon Guindon, Avery T. Willis Jr., and Bill Krause. 2010. *Real-Life Discipleship Training Manual: Equipping Disciples Who Make Disciples*. Colorado Spring, CO: NavPress.
A companion book to *Real-Life Discipleship*.

Reinsborough, Patrick and Doyle Canning. 2010. *RE:Imagining Change: How to Use Story-Based Strategy to Win Campaigns, Build Movements, and Change the World*. Oakland, CA: PM Press.
How does one instigate change these days? *RE:Imagining Change* suggests that this is best done by creating a story that alters people's perception of the subject we desire to see change in.

Richardson, Don. 1984. *Eternity in Their Hearts*. Ventura, CA: Regal Books.
Taking a close look at the ruins of Machu Picchu (an ancient Inca civilization), this book illustrates how the concept of one almighty God extends back over centuries and has been prevalent in a multitude of civilizations.

Sachs, Jonah. 2012. *Winning the Story Wars*. Boston, MA: Harvard Business Review Press.
A book on how stories are used in media today in order to reach us through the din of ads and other business spiels. Spoiler alert! Sachs uses the new word *digitoral* in describing how our culture and businesses relate to the mass media we experience every day.

Sanchez, Daniel R., J.O. Terry and LaNette W. Thompson. 2008. *Bible Storying for Church Planting*. Fort Worth, TX: Church Starting Network.
Bible storying is being used increasingly for evangelism and Christian nurture. This book takes a forward step in showing how it can be used in the exciting opportunity of starting new congregations. J.O. Terry also has a series of works in this regard in the Church Starting Network (CSN).

Scarborough, Lynn W. 2009. *Talk like Jesus*. Mumbai: Jaico Publishing House.

Schrag, Brian. 2013. *Creating Local Arts Together: A Manual to Help Communities Reach Their Kingdom Goals*. Pasadena, CA: William Carey Library.
A thoroughly useful book to bring creativity, communities, and the arts alive!

Schrag, Brian and Paul Neeley, eds. 2007. *All the World Will Worship: Helps for Developing Indigenous Hymns*. 3rd ed. Duncanville, TX: EthnoDoxology Publications.
A comprehensive book on both embracing worship through indigenous music as well as further developing such styles.

Shaw, Daniel. 1988. *Transculturation*. Pasadena, CA: William Carey Library.
Examines how culture comes into play during communication and translation.

Sheard, Daniel. 2007. *An Orality Primer for Missionaries*. Amazon Digital Services.
A much referred to self-published book is a quick read for anyone who wishes to understand orality; this resource will help people to think about how to minister.

So, Damon. 2006. *Jesus Revelation of His Father: A Narrative-Conceptual Study of the Trinity with special reference to Karl Barth* Milton Keynes: Paternoster.
With references to the Gospel of Matthew, this book examines the nature of the trinity in an original approach.

_____. 2010. *The Forgotten Jesus and the Trinity You Never Knew*. Eugene, OR: Wipf and Stock.
Provides a balanced examination of Jesus' life, ministry, death, and resurrection and how important aspects of his relationship with the Father and the Holy Spirit were present during those times.

Sogaard, Viggo. 1986. *Applying Christian Communication*. Ann Arbor, MI: University Microfilms.
Speaks on an important subject that is relevant across cultures and generations.

_____. 1993. *Media in Church and Mission*. Pasadena, CA: William Carey Library.
Written prior to much of the revolution in digital media, this book provides useful, strategic input for those involved in media and scripture engagement.

Spangler, Ann and Lois Tverberg. 2009. *Sitting at the Feet of Jesus: How the Jewishness of Jesus Can Transform Your Faith*. Grand Rapids, MI: Zondervan.
A rich exploration into Judaism, enriching our understanding of the context that Jesus was in, thereby giving us a better appreciation and understanding of the things he said and taught.

Spence, Jonathan D. 1985. *The Memory Palace of Matteo Ricci*. New York: Penguin Books.
Conveys the collision of two worlds: Counter-Reformation Europe and Ming China by telling the story of Jesuit Priest Matteo Ricci. Religiously and emotionally deep.

Sprenger, Marilee. 1999. *Learning and Memory: The Brain in Action*. Association for Supervision & Curriculum Development.
A close look at the brain and how it holds our memories.

Steffen, Tom A. 2005. *Reconnecting God's Story to Ministry: Crosscultural Storytelling at Home and Abroad*. Waynesboro, GA: Authentic Media.
Steffen helps readers see the value of storytelling for evangelism-discipleship. The book provides practical help by identifying the roles and tasks necessary to become an effective storyteller in another culture.

Thiselton, Anthony C. 2009. *Hermeneutics: An Introduction*. Grand Rapids, MI: William B. Eerdmans Publishing Co.
The author brings together a historical survey of hermeneutical approaches, as well as the development of last century's various theories, including reader-response and reception theory, and context of postmodernity.

Thompson, LaNette W. 1998. *The Nonliterate and the Transfer of Knowledge in West Africa* (Master's thesis). Retrieved from ProQuest Dissertations and Theses Database. (UMI No. 1391502)

_____. 1996, 2003. *Sharing the Message through Storying*. Burkina Faso: International Mission Board. Available at https://www.oralitystrategies.org/resources.cfm?id=384&t=13.

Thomas, Rosalind. 1989. *Oral Tradition and Written Record in Classical Athens*. Cambridge, UK: Cambridge University Press.
Writing and spoken word both hold great power separately, but what about when they are together? This book shows the relationship between the two and what influence they hold combined.

Trousdale, Jerry. 2012. *Miraculous Movements*. Nashville, TN: Thomas Nelson.
Touching stories of how God has worked in the lives of Muslims in Africa, revealing to us how we might become better at reaching out and sharing the gospel.

Tsering, Marku. 1988. *Sharing Christ in the Tibetan Buddhist World*. Upper Darby, PA: Tibet Press.
The author shares how Christians desiring to enter into the Tibetan Buddhist World can better relate to that culture as well as identify valuable elements in it that could lend to their own spiritual cultivation.

Walk Thru The Bible. 2011. *Story Thru The Bible: An Interactive Way to Connect with God's Word*. Colorado Sprints, CO: NavPress.
This approach to storying began in the 1980s. It uses word pictures and images to tell the whole story of the Bible. The WTB materials are translated into many languages, helping to train many people in OT and NT material. See more http://www.walkthru.org/where-we-work.

Walsh, John. 2003. *The Art of Storytelling: Easy Steps to Presenting an Unforgettable Story*. Chicago: Moody Press.
Many people dread the prospect of public speaking—Walsh writes from experience to help others overcome these fears, as he himself became a preacher despite his own fears.

Walton, John H. 2010. *The Bible Story Handbook: A Resource for Teaching 175 Stories from the Bible*. Wheaton, IL: Crossway Publishers.
An invaluable resource on teaching young children difficult stories in the Bible.

Werner, Dietrich, David Esterline, Namsoon Kang, and Joshua Raja. 2010. *Handbook of Theological Education in World Christianity*. Oxford: Regnum Books International.
This book holds over 90 expert contributions on recent developments in Christian theological education and contains regional surveys of ecumenical and denominational trends and models in theological education conducted on every continent.

Wiher, Hannes. 2003. *Shame and Guilt: A Key to Cross-Cultural Ministry*. Germany: Culture and Science Publication.
A biblical theological perspective on worldview studies and the discipline of orality. Resources available in both German and English.

Wilhoit, James C. 2008. *Spiritual Formation as if the Church Mattered: Growing in Christ through Community*. Grand Rapids, MI: Baker Academic.
Rather than focusing on the individual's spiritual transformation, this book concentrates on how the Church itself is the root of spiritual growth.

Willard, Dallas. 1991. *The Spirit of the Disciplines*. San Francisco: Harpercollins.
Timeless classic to read and reflect.

Willis, Avery T. Jr., and Mark Snowden. 2010. *Truth That Sticks: How to Communicate Velcro Truth in a Teflon World*. Colorado Springs, CO: NavPress.
From the unreached billions among oral cultures around the world, these authors bring oral communication strategy home to propose a small group model of discipling through the orality preferences all of us have in common.

Willis, Avery T. Jr., and Matt Willis. 2009. *Learning to Soar: How to Grow through Transitions and Trials*. Colorado Springs, CO: NavPress.
As a mother eagle prompts her young to get out of the nest and fly, so God prompts us, nudging us towards spiritual growth. This book moves us to respond to God's prompts.

Winter, Ralph. 1969. *Theological Education by Extension*. South Pasadena: William Carey Library.

Woodberry, Dudley J. 2008, 2011. *From Seed to Fruit: Global Trends, Fruitful Practices, and Emerging Issues among Muslims.* Pasadena, CA: William Carey Library.
A landmark study, highly recommended for anyone interested in how God is working among the Muslim people today.

Wright, Christopher J.W. and Jonathan Lamb, eds. 2009. *Understanding and Using the Bible.* London: SPCK Publishing.
This book explores Christian belief about the Bible and how to use and apply our knowledge of the Bible in a variety of contexts ranging across cultures and social settings.

Wright, N. T. 1992. *The New Testament and the People of God.* Minneapolis, MN: Augsburg Fortress Publishers.
One of five volumes that addresses theological questions on the origins of Christianity. This volume focuses on first-century Palestinian Judaism and contains excellent cultural and historical insights.

Zuck, Roy B. 2002. *Teaching as Jesus Taught.* Eugene, OR: Wipf and Stock.
Instead of focusing entirely on *what* Jesus taught, Zuck puts the emphasis on *how* Jesus taught and engaged his audience. Zuck suggests that we might apply such tactics to how we share our faith and pass on his message.

Periodicals and Journals

"Arts in Mission." 2010. *Connections, Journal of the WEA Mission Commission* 9(2-3). Special double issue, 1-98. Visit http://www.worldea.org/images/wimg/files/Arts in Mission.pdf for PDF.

Bandura, Albert. 2007. "Much Ado over a Faulty Conception of Perceived Self-efficacy Grounded in Faulty Experimentation." *Journal of Social and Clinical Psychology* 26: 641-658.

Bowen, Earle A. and Dorothy N. Bowen. 1988. "Contextualization of Teaching Methodology Is Theological Education in Africa." Paper presented at the Accrediting Council for Theological Education Conference of Theological Educators. ERIC 315 382.
The presented paper can be accessed at http://www.eric.ed.gov/ERICWebPortal/search/detailmini.jsp?_nfpb=true&_&ERICExtSearch_SearchValue_0=ED315382&ERICExtSearch_SearchType_0=no&accno=ED315382.

Brown, Rick. 2004. "Communicating Effectively to Non-Readers." *International Journal of Frontier Missions* 21(4): 173-178.

_____. 2004. "Communicating God's Message in an Oral Culture." *International Journal of Frontier Missions* 21(3): 122-128.
Based upon his extensive experiences in Africa and Asia, and in Bible translation and consulting, Brown examines core principles for communicating biblical truth in primarily oral cultures. He describes the way oral and print cultures learn and communicate, and the implications on the communication of biblical truth, as well as how the Bible readily lends itself to primarily oral cultures.

Chenoweth, Vida and Bee, Darlene. 1968. "On Ethnic Music." *Practical Anthropology.* 15(5): 205-212.

Chiang, Samuel E. 2009. "Oral Communicators and the Gospel." Connections, *Journal of the WEA Mission Commission* 8(2): 34.

_____. 2009. "Strategic Options for Back to Jerusalem." *Connections, Journal of the WEA Mission Commission* 8(3): 30-33.

_____. 2010. "The Oral Reality: Reaching and Discipling Oral Learners." *Congress Handbook.* Tokyo, 128-126.
Visit http://www.tokyo2010.org/resources/Tokyo2010_T2_Samuel_Chiang.pdf for the PDF.

Evans, Steve A . 2008. "From Biblical Worldview to Buddhist Worldview: Using Biblical Narratives to Impact at the Heart Level." DeNeui, Paul H., ed. *Communicating Christ Through Story and Song: Orality in Buddhist Contexts.* Pasadena, CA: William Carey Library. Chapter 6, 128-150.
Visit http://www.weaconnections.com/Back-issues/China.aspx for the PDF.

_____. 2009. "Using the Bible in Oral Cultures" *Understanding and Using the Bible.* Edited by Christopher J. W. Wright, and Jonathan Lamb. London: SPCK Publishing. Chapter 8, 122-137.

_____. 2009. "Media's Role in (Re)Shaping the Values of Today's Urban Buddhist and Its Impact on Gospel Proclamation" *Communicating Christ in Asian Cities: Urban Issues in Buddhist Contexts.* Edited by Paul H. De Neui. Pasadena, CA: William Cary Library. Chapter 2, 41-71.

_____. 2010. "Matters of the Heart: Orality, Story and Cultural Transformation— The Critical Role of Storytelling in Affecting Worldview." *Missiology* 38(2): 185-199.
This article proposes that worldview, culture, and values can be changed, resulting in the transformation of the individual as well as the culture to which he/she belongs.

_____. 2010. "The Impact of Cultural Folklore on National Values: A Preliminary Study with a Focus on Bhutan." *Storytelling, Self, Society: An Interdisciplinary Journal of Storytelling Studies* 6(1): 8-18.

_____. 2013. "'You Think in Lines, We Think in Circles": Oral Communication Implications in the Training of Indigenous Leaders' *Developing Indigenous Leaders: Lessons in Mission from Buddhist Asia.* Edited by Paul H. De Neui. Pasadena, CA: William Cary Library. Chapter 2, 21-37
A. Steve Evans work in Bhutan and across Asia provides observations and insights for us.

Green, Ron. 2010. "The Oral Story Bible: A Breakthrough Strategy in Oral Scripture Translation." Congress Handbook. Tokyo, 137-141.
Visit http://www.tokyo2010.org/resources/Handbook.pdf for more.

International Journal of Frontier Missions special 1995 issue on Reaching Non Literate Peoples 12(3). Available for download at http://www.ijfm.org/archives. htm.
Articles Include:
> Dependence on Literacy Strategy, Herb V. Klem
> The Crucial Role of Oral-Scripture, Gilbert Ansre
> The Emergence of Audio-Scripture in Church and Mission, Viggo Sogaard
> Audio-Communications and the Progress of the Gospel, Allan Starling
> Was Jesus a Zairian? Paul D. Dyer
> The Role of the O.T. in Evangelism, Don Pederson
> Storying the Storybook to Tribals, Tom A. Steffen

Authors speak on the complex task of communicating the gospel to people in ethnolinguistic groups who cannot read or do not depend on printed materials.

International Journal of Frontier Missions special 2011 issue on The Terms of Translation 28(3). Available for download at http://www.ijfm.org/archives.htm.
Articles Include:
> A New Look at Translating Familial Biblical Terms, Rick Brown Leith Gary, and Adrea Gray
> A Brief Analysis of Filial and Paternal Terms in the Bible, Rick Brown, Leith Gary, and Andrea Gray
> When "Literal" is Inaccurate: A Multi-Dimensional Approach to Translating Scripture Meaningfully, Donna Toulmin
> Ideological Challenges for Bible Translators, Roy E. Ciampa
> Basic Principles and Procedures for Bible Translation, Forum of Bible Agencies International

Authors deal with the complex subject of languages, worldview, and translations.

Krabill, James R. 2008. "Encounters: What Happens to Music When People Meet," in *Music in the Life of the African Church*. Edited by Roberta King, Jean Kidula, James R. Krabill, and Thomas Oduro, 57-79. Waco, TX: Baylor University Press.

Lovejoy, Grant. 2007. "The Extent of Orality," *Dharma Deepika: A South Asian Journal of Missiological Research* 25: 24-34. Republished online in the 2008 *Journal of Baptist Theology and Ministry* 5: 121-134.
This journal aims to integrate theology, history, anthropology, sociology, religious, and worldview studies and other aspects of missiological research.

Moon, W. Jay. 2012. "Rituals and Symbols in Community Development." *Missiology* 40(2): 141-153.
This journal is a forum for missiologists to exchange ideas and research.

_____. 2012. "Holistic Discipleship: Integrating Community Development in the Discipleship Process." *Evangelical Missions Quarterly* 48(1): 16-22.
EMQ houses cross-cultural writers who explore key topics in world missions today.

_____. 2012. "Understanding Oral Learners." *Teaching Theology and Religion* 15(1): 29-39.
This journal publishes articles that address various theological and religious issues of today.

Noss, Philip A. 1981. "The Oral Story and Bible Translation." *The Bible Translator* 27: 301-318.

"Orality." 2010. *Missiology: An International Review* 38(2): 107-242 View http://www.asmweb.org/content/home.

Orality Journal. 2012. 1(1).

_____. 2013. 2(1).

Prior, Randall. 2011. "Orality: Not-So-Silent Issue in Mission Theology." *International Bulletin of Missionary Research* 35(3): 143-147. View http://www.internationalbulletin.org/system/files/2011-03-143-prior.html.

"Redeeming the Arts: The Restoration of the Arts to God's Creational Intention." *Lausanne Occasional Paper*, no. 46. Accessed at www.lausanne.org/documents/2004forum/LOP46_IG17.pdf.

Roper, Don. 1983. "What is Group Media?" *WACC Journal*. London: World Association of Christian Communication.

Schrag, Brian. 2007. "Why Local Arts are Central to Mission." *International Journal of Frontier Missiology* 24(4): 199-202.

Smith, Pamala D. 2006. "Visual Art and Orality." *Unpublished paper*. Can be accessed at https://www.oralitystrategies.org/files/1/290/Visual Art and Orality.pdf.

Steffen, Tom A. 1994. "A Narrative Approach to Communicating the Bible, Part 1." *Christian Education Journal* 24: 86-97.

_____. 1994a. "A Narrative Approach to Communicating the Bible, Part 2." *Christian Education Journal* 24: 98-109.

_____. 1994b. "Paradigm Changes for Effective Evangelism." *Evangelism: A Lausanne Cooperating Periodical* 9: 136-140.

Sparks, Barbara. and Shauna. Butterwick. 2004. "Culture, Equity, and Learning." In *Dimensions of Adult Learning: Adult Education and Training in a Global Era*. Edited by G. Foley, 276-290. Crows Nest, Australia: Allen & Unwin.

Steffen, Tom A. and J.O. Terry. 2007. "The Sweeping Story of Scripture Taught Through Time." *Missiology: An International Review* 35(3): 315-335. Steffen and Terry give a carefully-researched run both through the current orality history (with excellent bibliographic information) and how leaders throughout history used oral methods.

Tsang, Sam. 2009. "Are We 'Misreading' Paul? Oral Phenomena and Their Implication for the Exegesis of Paul's Letters." *Oral Tradition*, 24(1): 205-225. The article provides a profound and insightful look at oral cultures and Paul's writings; an important resource can be found at http://journal.oraltradition.org/authors/show/534.

Turner, Harold W. 1967. "A Typology of Modern African Religious Movements." *Journal of Religion and Religions* 1(1): 1-34.

The following selected websites are grouped for specific interests within the subject of orality:

Praying and Informing

www.ethne.net/
www.finishingthetask.com
www.imb.org/globalresearch/
www.peoplegroups.org
thecall.com

Strategy and Informational

www.biblicalperformancecriticism.org/
conversation.lausanne.org/
en.wikipedia.org/wiki/Orality
www.echothestory.com/
www.heartstories.info
www.internationaloralitynetwork.com
www.mislinks.org/index.php?cID=836
www.oralstrategies.org
www.orality.net
orvillejenkins.com/orality/index.html
www.scripture-engagement.org/
www.themissionexchange.org/downloads/eXcelerate09.pdf
Abney, Lynne L. 2010. Orality Assessment Tool 2001 Available from
fjseries.org/low/Orality_Assessment_Tool_Worksheet.pdf.

Music and Arts

"Sounds of Global Worship"—the YouTube Channel for Heart Sounds International: www.YouTube.com/user/HSIOM
GIAL World Arts courses: www.gial.edu/dpt-langdev/world-arts.html
Heart Sounds International (HSI) www.heart-sounds.org
International Council of Ethnodoxologists (ICE) www.worldofworship.org

Training Curriculum and Deploying Teams with a Focus on the Unreached

208.109.43.65/
www.cbstorying.org
www.churchstarting.net/biblestorying/Books.htm
www.e3partners.org/orality
www.fjseries.org/low/home.html
www.freedomtolead.net/

nextgen4god.com/
www.OneStory.org
www.simplythestory.com
www.siutraining.org
www.storyrunners.com
www.visualstorybible.org
www.water.cc

Story Sets for Storytelling

www.bibletelling.org/
www.oralstrategies.org
www.orality.net
www.st4t.org
www.ywamonestory.org

Focusing on Women

www.projecthannah.org/about/
www.orality.net
www.siutraining.org

Church-planting Resources

www.churchplantingmovements.com/
www.miaoupg.com/
www.siutraining.org

Media Strategies and Content Distribution

www.faithcomesbyhearing.com/pastors-support-materials
http://www.davarpartners.com/
www.T4Global.org
www.twr.org

Indigenous Media Strategies and Tools

www.createinternational.com
www.indigitech.net

Secondary Oral Learners and Discipleship

bible4children.org/
www.cbs4kids.org
www.christianstorytelling.com
www.churchstarting.net/biblestorying/
www.combarriers.com/CommunicationStyles

crupressgreen.com/the-essentials/
www.dna-21.org
www.echothestory.com
www.globalshortfilmnetwork.com
www.ntmbooks.com/chronological_teaching
www.orality.net
www.reallifeministries.com
www.simplythestory.org
www.story4all.com/
www.storyseminary.com/
www.truthsticks.org
www.walkthru.org

Index